Evelyn Juers | The Recluse

Evelyn Juers

GIRAMONDO

The Recluse

First published 2012
from the Writing & Society Research Centre
at the University of Western Sydney
by the Giramondo Publishing Company
PO Box 752
Artarmon NSW 1570 Australia
www.giramondopublishing.com

Designed by Harry Williamson
Typeset by Andrew Davies
in 10/14. 5 pt Minion Pro
Printed and bound by SOS Print + Media
Distributed in Australia by NewSouth Books

National Library of Australia
Cataloguing-in-Publication data:

Juers, Evelyn, 1950–
The recluse / Evelyn Juers
ISBN 9781920882884 (pbk.)

920.72

for Indiana

On the Corner of King and Queen

As a student in the early 1970s I lived in a communal household in a large old Aegean-blue terrace at 5 Queen Street, in the inner Sydney suburb of Newtown. We read a lot, Freud and Marx and *The Golden Bough* and *The Female Eunuch*, played house, and Beethoven, smoked *Gauloises*, adopted a kitten. Often I'd stop on the corner of King and Queen, deciding whether to walk to classes at the university, where large lecture crowds made me feel queasy, or instead take my embroidered shoulder bag of nineteenth-century literature to Camperdown Cemetery and read there alone, in a circle of sun in winter, the deep shade of a tree in summer. One favourite spot was near the grave of Judge Donnithorne and his daughter Eliza. On those truant days when I'd had the courage to miss classes, and head down King Street towards the cemetery, I did not know I was passing the spot where the Donnithornes had lived and where Eliza had been a recluse for most of her adult life.

Much later I learnt that she was supposedly the model for Miss Havisham, the jilted bride in Charles Dickens' novel *Great Expectations* (1861). Dickens' protagonist Pip first encounters her *dressed in rich materials – satins, and lace, and silks – all of white. Her shoes were white. And she had a long white veil dependent from her hair, and she had bridal flowers in her hair, but her hair was white.* On closer inspection Pip sees that the flowers are withered and Miss Havisham is faded and yellow. She is the embodiment of anticipation and disappointment.

Great Expectations, which I read in a graveyard, begins in a graveyard. Central to the book's complex set of narratives, is the story of a wealthy witchlike spinster who lives in a ruined mansion, Satis House, with her adopted daughter Estella. She is in her mid-fifties but seems ancient; her wealth is inherited; her private tragedy is that she had once fallen in love with a man called Compeyson, a swindler who jilted her on her wedding day. Shocked, she had all the clocks in her house stopped at the time of her betrayal, and froze herself as a bride-in-waiting, always in her wedding dress, one shoe off, one shoe on, the wedding cake uneaten. She required revenge. In a grotesque plagiarism of motherhood, she *wanted a little girl to rear and love, and save from my fate*, intending to steal *her heart away and put ice in its place*. She tested Estella's iciness on boys like Pip. Estella would break their hearts, as hers, Miss Havisham's, had once been broken. To say more would be to spoil the story for anyone who hasn't read it, and in its elaborate round-aboutness, test the patience of those who know it well. It's enough to say the narrative begins coldly – Dickens being the master of shivering, toe-biting British winter coldness – and finishes warmly. Pirouettes of fortune link up the characters' nastinesses, genialities, and genealogies. The bleak Kentish marshes are overlaid with the streets of London, and with New South Wales, though the latter is merely a plot device. Finally there's a fire, forgiveness, two possible endings and the book itself: *Great Expectations* is Dickens' greatest achievement. Pip and Estella and the other characters, Magwitch, Drummle, Wopsle and the Pockets, to name a few, for all their spark, are secondary to Miss Havisham, who rules in the history of literature like a queen.

Dickens did not disclose much about his conception of Miss Havisham. But it's generally agreed that this archetype of the thwarted bride had a number of prototypes. One was Elizabeth Parker, of Newport, Shropshire, whose life is said to have taken a similar turn to Miss Havisham's; Dickens heard about her when he visited Newport, where he stayed at Havisham Court. Then there were women who behaved madly and wore white, whom Dickens encountered when he wandered around London as a boy, including the White Woman of Berners Street. There was Lady Lytton, wife of Dickens' friend Bulwer-Lytton, placed by her husband in an asylum. This type also occupied the mind of Dickens' friend Wilkie Collins, whose sensational novel of female instability, *The Woman in White*, appeared in 1861. And there was the story of Martha Joachim. *Household Words*, the magazine Dickens edited in the 1850s, reported an inquest into Joachim's death in great detail: how her bull-dog savagely attacked the jury that had come to view the body, how years before her father was robbed and murdered in Regent's Park, and later her suitor *whom her mother rejected, shot himself while sitting on the sofa with her, and she was covered with his brains. From that instant she lost her reason.* Martha Joachim was described as a recluse who dressed in white, mollycoddled her bulldog and two cats, and lived in a house full of lead soldiers *which she called her 'body-guards'*; she died of bronchitis (or, her soldiers poisoned her). So quite apart from Eliza Emily Donnithorne, Dickens had plenty to work with.

Archetypes produce offspring. *Great Expectations* has been filmed at least seven times. Most memorably Jean Simmons, Anne Bancroft and Charlotte Rampling have played Miss Havisham, with Helena Bonham Carter in the latest film version. A recent BBC television series starred Gillian Anderson. Of her character Anderson is reported to have said, *She hasn't bathed for 18 years so I kept having images of that type of fungus which has frilly ends and I thought if we had that growing on my neck it could look amazing.* One of the most disturbing renditions is a poem by Carol Ann Duffy (British Poet Laureate since 2009), written in 1998 and titled 'Miss Havisham Mean Time'. Like a surgeon with a mind to murder, the poet puts *love's hate behind a white veil* and wants *a male corpse for a long slow honeymoon.* Duffy has subverted the myth of the Minotaur, her Miss Havisham is the monster.

Literary characters, like Miss Havisham, have elasticity, and no matter how much you stretch them to fit even your wildest adaptations, they always settle back into their original text. But Eliza Donnithorne was a real person and despite her renown – as eccentric recluse and possible Dickensian prototype – for her there is no text, no biography, only an untidy and questionable assortment of biographical facts and fictions.

Reclusion resists historical recovery. As it closes the door against the world, or in some cases leaves the door enticingly unlatched, reclusion also attracts voyeurism and ignites speculation. I began by wondering to what extent Eliza Donnithorne corresponded to, or had been subsumed by, Miss Havisham, but I was lured firmly in pursuit of her, not by any rumoured, gaudy eccentricity on her part, rather the opposite, by what one commentator called an *evanishment,* a term which implies, not absence, but an irretrievable presence. I was also intrigued by the possibility that she had been a reader in her reclusion, some say a *great* reader.

Paradoxically, the real and virtual sites where I went looking for this recluse – genealogies, newspapers, books, libraries, the internet, the history of the British in India, the towpaths of Twickenham, the polymorphous suburb of Newtown – these are all populous places. I found that reclusion happens within, not apart from, communalities. Like a soliloquy in a play. And it's in these busy social contexts that I've mined for direct, as well as indirect – adjacent, associative, suggestive, incidental – information about the unknown Eliza Emily Donnithorne.

Sketches for the Portrait of a Recluse

The Donnithornes came from the small town of St Agnes in Cornwall. *Burke's Landed Gentry* (1862) gives them a Spanish ancestor called Don Thoan, who was shipwrecked on the Cornish coast. Other sources suggest the name was originally De Bonython, an ancient family, one branch of which produced Sparkling Cornish Spring Water, from *deep below the rocky heart of Cornwall.* It seems more likely that the surname has a Celtic or Old English derivation. There was a Nicholas Donnithorne (1669–1737) whom documents describe c. 1704 as a Tin Blower; in 1731 he was a High Sheriff of Cornwall. He married Joanna (née Prideaux) in 1690; they had seven children.

One of their sons, Joseph Donnithorne (1691–1743), was lessee of the Polberro Mine. His brother, the Rev. Isaac Donnithorne (1709–1784) became his heir. An Anglican priest ordained in 1735, Isaac was a businessman, a clergyman and we might assume, a reader; in a portrait by Thomas Gainsborough he is surrounded by books and papers on a desk and shelves, with some very large volumes on the floor beside him.

Joanna was living at Trevellas Manor in St Agnes – where, I've been told, *the wind howls up from the coast* – with her unmarried daughter Elizabeth and son Joseph in the mid 1700s, when John Wesley rode his rounds of Methodist preaching. He stopped to preach at St Agnes *where all received the truth in love, except two or three who soon walked away*. Wesley returned two years later, in September 1757, *to find the great man, Mr Donnithorne was dead*, a reference to James, brother of Joseph and Elizabeth. Wesley was told about an earthquake that had occurred in July, *a rumbling noise under the ground hoarser and deeper than common thunder…a trembling of the earth* and a buckling of the ground on which they stood. He was inspired by Nature's fervour, for a *thundering sermon* was delivered at the church that Sunday. And he was impressed with old *Mrs Donythorne, who has her understanding entire, reads without spectacles, walks without a scarff and has scarce a wrinkle at ninety years of age…she is teachable as a child, and groaning for salvation.* Wesley was in full force; that year he published *The Doctrine of Original Sin: According to Scripture, Reason, and Experience.*

In the mid-eighteenth century, members of the Donnithorne family moved between London, where they were well-connected, and their homes in Cornwall. Isaac's daughter Penelope married Christopher Harris, who succeeded his uncle John Harris – he had served Kings George II and III – as master of the royal household; Isaac's son Nicholas was a Warden of the Stannaries (tin mines) of St Agnes to the Prince of Wales. He was involved in shipping tin from the Polberro mine to China, Bengal and Madras; in 1795 a contemporary described him as an *agent for the County and a gentleman of considerable wealth.* Nicholas was portrayed – in a brown coat with white fur lining – by a painter in the Circle of George Willison. He had married Anne (Anna)

Comyn, of Barker in Essex, and I've read that their London address was Coombe Hill House in Croydon; it's a large house, possibly they leased an apartment there. He died, in debt, in 1796. Nicholas and Anne were Eliza's grandparents; their second son James was her father. From his mother James later inherited her *very handsome diamond ring*.

James Donnithorne was born 2 April 1773, probably in London, but his exact place of birth is unknown. He was baptised at St Mary Aldermanbury, a church first destroyed in the Great Fire of London in 1666, rebuilt to a design by Christopher Wren, and destroyed again in the Blitz of 1940, its stones sold and the church reborn in Fulton, Missouri, USA.

In Cornwall, the family had once been confident enough of its wealth to build a summer house on St Agnes Beacon, the highest point in the district, part of a chain of coastal hilltops where flares could be lit to warn of invasion. At the base of the hill is an ancient earthwork called The Bolster, after a legendary giant, a married man who mistreated his wife by making her carry rocks in her apron to the top of the hill. Cornish legends of piskies, mermaids and giants must have been passed to each new generation of Donnithornes, especially the story of a local girl who emulated the Roman Saint Agnes, protector of chastity and virgins. As a young girl of twelve or thirteen Saint Agnes rejected a suitor and as punishment was raped, imprisoned, and burnt, which she survived. When she was beheaded it's said her blood flowed across the floor of the colosseum and was soaked up by Christians. Courted by the Bolster giant, who expressed his love by *filling the air with the tempest of his sighs and groans*, the Cornish Agnes challenged him to prove his worth by plugging a rockhole with his blood. The aptly named Bolster obliged, unaware the hole in a cave at nearby Chapel Porth was bottomless and drained into the sea. He died. A nineteenth-century collector of folklore Robert Hunt wrote, *The persecuted lady, finding there was no release for her, while this monster existed, resolved to be rid of him at any cost.* So she did what she did, and *thus the lady got rid of her hated lover; Mrs Bolster was released, and the district freed from the presence of a tyrant.* Tracks of blood-red stains in the cave are now less miraculously explained as iron ore deposits.

Eliza's father James Donnithorne named his first-born daughter Agnes, and one of his Australian properties St Agnes. But it seems it was his youngest daughter Eliza who took the story most to heart.

In India

Some say James spent his youth dissolutely and to avoid further ruin, around 1792, aged nineteen or twenty, he became a writer for the British East India Company, which had been established by Robert Clive for British predominance in Bengal.

In 1853 Karl Marx looked back at its history and saw that *the East*

India Company commenced attempting merely to establish factories for their agents, and places of deposit for their goods. In order to protect them they erected several forts, but *the events of the Seven-Years-War transformed the East India Company from a commercial into a military and territorial power*, creating an immense revenue system that brought exploitation and corruption.

After the Company's victory over the Nawab of Bengal and his French allies at the Battle of Plassey in 1757, the British continued to turn Indian rulers into vassals and to consolidate its powers across the sub-continent, including administrative power, the right to collect revenue, and to grant trade monopolies and exemptions. In 1772 it established Calcutta as the capital of India. By the mid-nineteenth century its rule extended across India, Burma, Malaya, Singapore, and British Hong Kong. It was all about trade: in cotton, raw silk, indigo dye, saltpetre, sugar cane, tea, and the opium poppies that grew so well in the alluvial soils along the Ganges.

It's been assumed (but I've seen no proof) that soon after James came to India to work for the Company, he met the merchant sea-captain William Wright Bampton and sought adventure on his ship *Shah Hormuzeer*, on a trading and charting voyage to Sydney, arriving there in February 1793. Bampton brought 110 Bengal sheep to the colony, and a cargo of food, including salted meats, flour, wheat and rice, as well as iron, nails and other building materials, and alcohol. In

June the *Hormuzeer*, and the *Chesterfield* captained by Matthew Alt, left for Norfolk Island and India. In his neatly written journal, Bampton noted that they intended to pass through Torres Strait *by a route which the Commanders did not know to have been before attempted.* They succeeded, but only with a great deal of guesswork and error. Their navigation was marred by murder and mayhem; occasionally they managed to hoist the Union Jack. David Collins, an early chronicler of events in and around the colony of New South Wales, describes men from the *Hormuzeer* and *Chesterfield* landing on an island *abounding with the red sweet potato, sugar cane, plantains, bamboo, cocoa trees, and mangroves*, where *the natives appeared stout*, and where Bampton lost a number of companions. When they looked for them, they discovered coats with buttons cut off, and *some incontestable proofs that their friends could not be living; of three human hands which they took up, one, by some particular marks, was positively thought…to have belonged to Mr Carter.* They returned to Bombay early in 1794. Trade between India and Australia was hazardous, but greatly encouraged. Bampton lost two ships, one in the Hooghly River with a cargo of cattle, another near New Zealand. He must have discussed the pros and cons with Captain Lachlan Macquarie, the Scottish-born British army officer and veteran of the American War of Independence, who had been in India since 1788 and succeeding William Bligh, would become Governor of NSW from 1810 until 1821. Macquarie and his first wife Jane dined with Bampton and his wife in Bombay on 20 May 1794. More dinners followed; the historian Robin Walsh tells me it was a lively and ever-changing social scene, and these two couples seemed to enjoy each other's company. The men were often away, Macquarie involved in military campaigns in southern India, and Bampton on his speculative voyages and maritime contracts to ferry troops to and from Bombay, and between British garrisons on the western coast of India. The following year he captained the *Endeavour* to Port Jackson, arriving in May with food and 130 cattle. He took the opportunity to buy land in Sydney and the Hunter Valley. In September 1795 he left Port Jackson with 50 emancipated convicts, and about as many stowaways. It was a perilous voyage. The ship was damaged during a gale and scuttled in Facile Harbour, Dusky Sound, New Zealand. Here the survivors found a partly built schooner, which they finished and named *Providence*, and leaving some men behind, sailed to Norfolk Island, where they dropped off the stowaways.

Bampton, born around 1756, was a Londoner, descended from instrument makers, shipwrights, street traders and barber-surgeons. He'd been a gunner's servant on the *Harcourt*, a seaman on the *Crook* and *Stormont*, midshipman on the *Earl Talbot*, second mate on the *Resolution*, third mate on the *Worcester*, second and first mate on the *Raymond*; he captained the *Jane*, *Shah Hormuzeer*, and *Endeavour*. He was a widower when he married Sarah Hussey in 1784, was declared bankrupt in 1790, and arrived in Bombay in July 1791, where he set himself up in the 'country trade'. His children include William Wright (1785) and Sarah Elizabeth (1787), William James (1797) and Richard Charles (1798). There's a portrait of William James Bampton in the State Library of NSW (until recently mistakenly thought to be a portrait of his father) which shows a handsome man with glasses.

William Bampton senior died 9 August 1813 in Calcutta, West Bengal. To his son William he left his gold watch; to Richard Charles a diamond brooch, a plain brooch, and sleeve buttons; his wife Sarah received everything else; his son-in-law James Donnithorne was one of his executors.

James Donnithorne had become Second Assistant to the Court of Appeal and Circuit at Patna by April 1794, rising to the position of First Assistant in 1796. Two years later he was Registrar at the chief court of appeal for civil matters in Jessore. James' son Henry was born in 1799, his daughter Agnes Ann was born in 1801; there was at least one other son, James Henry born around 1800. Uncertainty surrounds the identity of their mother(s). Henry's mother is listed as Sarah Bampton (which would not have been possible since Sarah was only 12 when he was born), while Agnes' mother has not been identified and may have died in childbirth in 1801. Old records are often incomplete or incorrect. We might guess that the mother of Henry and Agnes was not documented because she was Indian, or that they were illegitimate, or both. In March 1803, James became Collector at Nuddea and in January

1807 he became Acting Judge and Magistrate of Ramgarh (Ramghyr), with District headquarters at Chatra, where in the previous year the social activist and later leader of Bengal's cultural revolution, Raja Ram Mohan Roy, had been a sub-registrar. Perhaps they met briefly. It seems that this was the only time, from 1807 to 1808, that James held the position of judge, though he would later – in Australia – style himself as Judge James Donnithorne.

A month after he took up the appointment at Ramgarh, his daughter Agnes, aged six, accompanied by her uncle Captain William Comyn of the 17th native infantry, departed for England on the *Monarch*.

That year James Donnithorne, aged thirty-four, married the Captain's daughter Sarah Elizabeth Bampton, aged 20. They had seven children: William Sherson born in 1807, followed by Edward Harris in 1810, Charles Deane in 1812, Penelope in 1814, Catherine Maria in 1816, Arthur Rennel in 1818, and Eliza Emily in 1821. Charles and Arthur did not survive infancy.

In February 1808 James was appointed Collector and Mint Master of Farruckhabad and held this post until 1822. The family lived at nearby Fatehgarh, where he bought land at a good price in 1810, demolished an old house in 1814 and built a new one, lauded by Charles Lindsay Wallace in *Fatehgarh Camp 1777–1857* as *a habitation, which was the object of much admiration... The compound was entered through a large gate house. At the end of the drive was the mansion itself, described as very extensive and convenient. The garden around the house was laid out with shrubs and lawns. In front of it was a square tank, filled with 'red and green' fish, and with a fountain in the middle. A well, with Persian wheel attached, was another of the curiosities of the garden.*

In 1776 Captain Charles Marsack, natural son of George II by Marguerite de Marsack, had raised a cavalry regiment and established a British military encampment at Fatehgarh on the Ganges. It is now a town in Farrukhabad District, in the state of Uttar Pradesh. In Wallace's account of those early British times, we read of officers living in bungalows made of sun-dried bricks, with low grass-thatched roofs that resembled haystacks or beehives, which burnt easily when struck by lightning. Interiors were well lit and aired through wooden shutters. Servants brought silver trays with *tea, toddy, and water from the Ganges*, refreshments taken on verandahs that overlooked the river. Separate buildings housed kitchens and other *necessaries*. People attended suppers and dances, played card games and billiards or rehearsed theatricals: a favourite was Goldsmith's comedy of manners *She Stoops to Conquer*. Some – like the Donnithornes – lived in compounds surrounded with high mud walls, and kept gardens of fruit trees, vegetables and flowers. Nim trees provided shade near houses, and were planted along roads as avenues. Standing alone, or in groves, were mango trees, not just for fruit, but for construction of bridges and huts, as well as tamarind, goolar and shisham trees.

But it was not idyllic. Those who ventured unaccompanied beyond the fort and settlement and across the treeless kankar plain that stretched along the Ganges to the ravines near Rakha, had to fend off robbers and wolves. The heat was oppressive and when *the hot weather was in progress* (this is Wallace's constant phrase), it *roughened tempers* and people became ill, some died of sunstroke. Among the soldiers, discontent and ennui led to quarrels, duels and the threat of mutiny by sepoys over unpaid wages. A further worry for the community were the families of soldiers who had died in battle, left behind to fend for themselves in Fatehgarh. Wallace also tells of *some residents of an undesirable type* [who] *were in the habit of living in tents, which they pitched in odd places*, and gives the example of a drunkard, who died and was completely eaten up by ants. Roads were dusty in dry, then muddy in wet seasons. There were earthquakes, snakes, and too many stray dogs.

But roads and bridges and housing improved, a hospital, theatre and church were built, a greater range of provisions was imported, with a big demand for wine and beer. And soda water. The writer Emma Roberts recounts: *Until of late years, this refreshing beverage, which forms one of the greatest luxuries in a tropical climate, was imported from Europe and sold at a very high price; there is now a large establishment at Futyghur, which sends out supplies all over the country.*

People transported themselves on horseback, in palanquins and two-wheeled buggies, sometimes by elephant. The Ganges remained the main route in and out; in the early days it took about three months from Calcutta. People often travelled in fleets, with many barges servicing a single household on the move. The river was also *one of the usual diversions*, especially for *a very agreeable trip to Agra, Muttra and Delhi.* The Nawab of Farrukhabad's cession to the East India Company had brought collectors, judges and their assistants, chaplains and surgeons to the garrison and district, also an influx of indigo planters and cotton merchants, and workers for the clothing and gun-carriage factories. Many officers were traders, many had Indian wives. Fatehgarh bazaar, initially a collection of straw huts, became the social centre. For better services and goods – Kashmir shawls and other textiles, including gold and silver lace, precious stones, copper, brass and iron, borax from Hohilkhand, potatoes – you went to Farrukhabad.

As Collector and Master of the Mint, James Donnithorne oversaw the work of producing coins; he was in charge of purchases of charcoal and wood, and a team of blacksmiths, carpenters, refiners. He was proud of the beauty and precision of his Farrukhabad rupee. Wallace relates an incident in 1809, when Donnithorne *crossed the Ganges with a company of infantry in order to collect the revenue, and had to blow up a mud fort, which barred his way*, and a similar event in 1815; *Mr Donnithorne's assessment* [of revenue] *was extremely unpopular*. He was also Postmaster. Originally mail was delivered by a runner accompanied by drummers and torch bearers to frighten away the wild animals, then by postal waggon. Either way, due to embezzlement or attack, postal delivery was fraught. Sometimes Donnithorne complained to higher authorities about conditions and equipment; in 1812 he wanted his office tent replaced because it was too old. In a different light, he was a keen gardener who grew fruit and vegetables. Another of his hobbies was to make detailed miniature models of military equipment, such as cannons, complete with carriages. These he presented as gifts to visitors. He may well have given one to Francis Rawdon-Hastings, Lord Moira, who was in Fatehgarh in 1815.

Lord Moira had fought in the American War of Independence and the French Revolutionary Wars. He was on good terms with the Prince of Wales, who was Prince Regent from 1811 to 1820 and on the death of his father became George IV; his aristocracy of leisure, pleasure, cultural refinement and excess, was deeply shadowed by war, colonialism, and people's poverty and uprisings; he's patted on the back for civic improvements like the introduction of gaslights to the streets of London in 1814, and military triumphs like the defeat of Napoleon at the Battle of Waterloo in 1815. Representing king, prince and country, Lord Moira (later Marquess of Hastings) was the Governor-General of India. He kept a diary.

Of his approach to Futteghur (his spelling) on 10 March 1815, he thought *the country has been improving in appearance latterly…the whole plain, wherever the eye can reach, is covered with luxuriant crops,* including large groves of mango trees. But then it changed again to arid soil, ravines and roads through very narrow passes. Lord Moira's entourage – horses, elephants, carriages – included his military secretary, Persian interpreter, eight aides-de-camp and three reserves, doctor, chaplain, and British and native infantry and cavalry. It included his wife Flora Campbell, 6th Countess of Loudon, and their young children: Flora aged nine, George seven, Sophia six, Selina five, and Adelaide three, and personal attendants. And it included the Bengali artist Sita Ram, trained in Patna to paint in an Indo-European linear style and palette. He documented this tour of northern India in Arcadian watercolours of dreamy pleasant places and events.

At Fatehgarh the Governor-General immediately notes with satisfaction the mint *for converting into our coin the various moneys received*. His men pitched their camp on a parade ground near the theatre, and he established himself *in an excellent house, lent to us by Mr Donnithorne…it is very extensive and convenient*. A painting of the whole procession shows it arriving *during the Hot winds of 1815* in the landscaped clearing of the Donnithornes' new estate, built half a mile south-west of the fort. Another painting shows the house as a pink bungalow with light blue window shutters, shaded by nim trees, a scene easily animated, in my imagination, with figures busy behind screens, a ball, a dog, some children's voices. A white-breasted kingfisher flies up from the river and settles on a branch.

For more than five months the Donnithornes moved out and the Governor-General ruled the country from their house, commanding the Anglo-Nepalese War (1814–1816). There he received visitors, a constant stream. He's interested in wildlife, so they bring him a live lizard, a preserved cobra, an *ichneumon* or Indian Gray Mongoose, some black scorpions, a wolf. He hears about many children, and some women, taken by wolves, *which come after dark into the very houses*, and that locals would not kill wolves for fear of the animal's revenge. He gave luxurious breakfasts to distinguished visitors, like the Nawab of Farrukhabad, who enjoyed strawberries and *a quantity of peaches* sent by Mr Donnithorne from his garden. With extravagant ceremony he returns their visits.

Celebrations for the King's birthday on 4 June 1815 were cancelled due to hot winds; when fireworks were held in the parade ground in the evening, *the air and the ground were of a temperature almost intolerable.* Ram depicts *illuminations and fireworks round Mr Donnithorne's park* on the cooler evening of 12 August, the Prince Regent's birthday, the garden lit with 50,000 lamps made of little earthenware cups filled with oil and grass wicks, raised all around on bamboo frames; it was thought the fireworks were *tolerably good, but not with the variety common in Europe*; the display was followed by supper. Lord Moira left on 22 August, sailing for Cawnpore. He was satisfied with *the conduct of those persons in their several stations under Government, and…impressed with the strongest sense of their upright and active discharge of their duties.* He was sad to leave; the chronicler Wallace comments that *his regret was probably exceeded by the delight of the Collector in getting back his own house after five months dispossession.* Wallace thought Mr Donnithorne would later have retired to a peaceful old age in Cornwall, where he *must often have recalled this spot to his memory, a home of which not a vestige of its former magnificence now remains.*

Were the Donnithornes a happy family? Did their colonial life make perfect sense to them?

At home in Fatehgarh in April 1818, James' daughter Agnes, nearly seventeen, married Henry Swetenham, aged twenty-six, her father's Assistant Collector. The chaplain at Cawnpore, Rev. Evans, had come to perform the ceremony.

From 1818 to the mid-1820s they lived through a cholera epidemic, which by some estimates had killed almost a third of Lord Moira's army; soldiers were both spreaders and victims of the disease. Did it also take the life of the Donnithorne's son Arthur Rennel? He was not quite a year old when he died in 1819. James Donnithorne also became ill that year, not from cholera, but (according to a later letter) from extreme fatigue and *from the pernicious effects of the numerous furnaces he was compelled to superintend in the two departments of the Mint,* which *led to the loss of the use of his limbs.* Soon after, in January 1820, Mrs Donnithorne and one child went to England on the East Indiaman *Prince Blucher*;

perhaps she was taking one of their sons to school. In July the same year, Mr and Mrs Donnithorne and two children, presumably their daughters Penelope and Catherine Maria, about six and four, travelled again on the *Prince Blucher* to the Cape of Good Hope, where James hoped to recover from his illness; but he dutifully returned to India on *The Surrey* in August. In 1821 the Donnithornes were living at 59 Loop Street, Cape Town.

Eliza Emily Donnithorne was born 9 July 1821 at Cape of Good Hope and baptised later that year on 2 October at St George's Cathedral, Cape Town.

Born there the previous year – according to an announcement, *in the house of friends of her parents named Donnithorne* – was Sarah Eliza Donnithorne Shakespear, always called Selina. As an infant she returned to Calcutta with her parents. William Makepeace Thackeray was her cousin. In a family memoir *Fifty Years with John Company*, Ursula Low (related to the Shakespears and Thackerays) recounts the heartbreaking separation of parents, especially mothers, and children, when these were sent to school or to live with relatives in Britain. *Such partings – always the bitterest portion of the British lot in India – were more cruel in times when all the days of childhood had to run their course before the possibility of reunion.* Soon after Selina's birth, Emily Shakespear said goodbye to her daughters Charlotte, aged seven, and Marianne, just four. They would never see their parents again. At sea, Marianne was given a letter from her mother, which remained her lifelong treasure: *My beloved Marianne, I send you a little parcel because I think it will please you to receive it from your mother… Poor old Ayah has been crying sadly for you both, sweet love. Your mother can think of nothing but her two darling little girls, & would give the world to give you once more a kiss & take her sweet little Marianne once more in her arms…*

In 1823 *Mrs Donnithorne and child* (Eliza was aged between one and two) and *James Donnithorne, Esq. of the Civil Service*, returned to Calcutta on the *Princess Charlotte*. James became Collector of Bullooah. Their son William was at East India College at Haileybury in Hertfordshire, learning languages (the school offered Sanskrit, Bengali, Arabic and Persian), law, political economy, mathematics and natural philosophy, classical and general literature, in training for the overseas civil service.

That year the Supreme Court at Calcutta, with Sir Antony Buller the presiding judge, assessed the damages (laid at 100,000 rupees) of the case Swetenham v. Macnaghten. It concerned the *criminal conversation* – adultery – of James' married daughter Agnes Ann Swetenham, now aged 22, *beautiful and accomplished*, and mother of a son not quite four years old. Through the transcript of the court case, we enter the family domain, obliquely, with glimpses of detail far back in time.

According to the Advocate-General, the Swetenhams lived at Fatehgarh *with a harmony and affection seldom equalled*:

The father of the lady will tell you, that if his son-in-law had any fault, as a husband, it was that he was too indulgent, that he was so fond of his wife that he humoured her in every whim, in every caprice, and in every extravagance. It will be shown that they continued to live together in this affection, until this destroyer, the defendant, came to blast their honour and happiness.

Mr Swetenham met Lieutenant Robert Macnaghten, who was also Deputy-Judge Advocate General, on a visit to Cawnpore in September 1822. With his *very fascinating* manners, Macnaghten charmed Swetenham, who invited him to visit at Fatehgarh. Macnaghten arrived in October, Mr Swetenham was absent, but expecting the visitor had left instructions with his brother-in-law to receive him. When he returned, and immediately had to leave again, he asked the visitor to come too:

The defendant and a Mr. Mangles accompanied Mr. and Mrs. Swetenham on this journey into the district; they travelled in tents, and my client was under the necessity of going daily to his Kutcheri, at some distance from the tents in the discharge of the multifarious and pressing duties imposed on him in the management of a large district, and of remaining until late in the afternoon. The defendant occupied a tent near that of Mr. Mangles.

But Mr Mangles had to return to Fatehgarh and one day around noon Mr Swetenham's servant thought he heard someone calling him from the dining tent; when he got there, *the dishonour of my client was completed.* When questioned, the servant *swore directly to have witnessed adultery* and that *they both got angry with me, and I went out.* Fearful of the consequences, the servant kept it secret from his master, who by all accounts was very fond of his wife. The servant said, I *am a black man; how could I dare to say so? If I had, he would have taken my life from me.* Two or three days later, he saw *the lady in a great chair sitting on the gentleman's knees, with her arm over his neck…And so it turned out that this intercourse went on, and has continued up to the present time.* Everyone returned to Fatehgarh together, but Swetenham, *too noble* for any suspicions, had to leave once more for Cawnpore. It's suggested that the defendant then *laid a dawk for two persons*, intending to elope with Mrs Swetenham. Their plans were interrupted by her brother-in-law and neighbour, Captain Adonia Smith, who was alerted by servants. He *found Mrs Swetenham dressed and leaning over her child which was asleep in a cot. I asked her what was the matter, that she was out of bed at that time of night.* She appeared distressed. He and other family members persuaded her to go back to bed. It was discovered that some of her belongings were already on the boat on the Ganges, hired by Macnaghten. Smith then carried Agnes *by force* to his bungalow, where she made two attempts to escape. Meanwhile her husband was told and immediately returned. He refused to see his wife ever again, offered to pay her an allowance of 300 rupees a month, and said she could live anywhere she wanted, in England or India, on the condition that she lived alone. She considered his proposal, and then obtained a boat, saying it was too late for her to change her course of action.

Defending Macnaghten, Mr Money said his client was deeply repentant and requested no word to be said against Mr Swetenham. He asked only for mitigation of damages, since he had not practised any *arts of seduction* and never intended *to ensnare and betray*. Mr Money suggests Mrs Swetenham was always *forward*, therefore it was her fault. *My client is as sorry as any man can be for the crime he has committed; there is only one excuse for him; he is a young man, and he is left in a tent alone with a young and beautiful woman*...a situation in which *a very large portion of mankind would have been unable to resist the extraordinary temptation* to which his client was exposed. Mr Money then argues that his client does not have the means to pay the amount proposed, that if heavy damages are awarded, he would have to go to gaol. This is what Judge Buller decided:

The only thing like an argument in mitigation is, that the lady may have fallen too easily, that she did not make that resistance which might have been expected in her case. But when it was considered that she was only twenty-one years of age, and the defendant, according to evidence, thirty,

I think that even this argument falls to the ground, and that the damages I have made up my mind to give will not be thought excessive... Under all the circumstances, therefore, I pronounce a verdict for the plaintiff – damages, Twelve Thousand Rupees – (Fifteen Hundred Pounds sterling.)

First *the unfortunate lady* lived *not in happiness... with her seducer*, then the Swetenhams got back together. Of Henry Swetenham, a Commissioner in 1832–34, a Civil and Sessions Judge 1835–41, Wallace said that he *appears to have been of a fiery nature*, never without a silver tray of cardamon, who enjoyed the refreshment of a *dali* of rose water, oranges, and pomegranates, and smoked a *huqqa* in court. Their son Henry Donnithorne Swetenham, born 1819 in Fatehgarh, was educated in England at Rugby, under the headmastership of Dr Arnold, one of Lytton Strachey's Eminent Victorians. Like his uncles William and Edward Donnithorne, he served in the 16th Lancers, a cavalry regiment of the British Army; he became a lieutenant, and was killed in action against Sikh forces at the battle of Aliwal on 28 January 1846, described by its jubilant commander Sir Harry Smith as *one of the most glorious battles ever fought in India*. Agnes and Henry also had two daughters, one of whom, Jane Penelope, born 1826 in Fatehgarh, was married a few months after her brother's death in 1846, to Anthony Charles Herring, at the Old Church, Fort William, Calcutta; they had two daughters and she died aged twenty-four in 1850 in Bombay. Together Mr and

Mrs H. Swetenham travelled to England in the 1840s and 50s. Henry died about 1860. In the census of 1871, Agnes was living in London, at Blomfield Terrace, Paddington, with three servants, and an income from dividends.

The seducer Robert Adair Macnaghten (born 1796 in Antrim, Ireland) was no ordinary scoundrel. After his escapade with Agnes, he married a young widow, Laura Henrietta Newport (née Roberts) in London in 1827. Her sister, who accompanied the couple to India, was the writer Emma Roberts, a close friend of the poet and novelist Letitia Landon, who had been briefly engaged to Dickens' close friend and biographer, John Forster. They lived in Agra, Cawnpore and Etawah, where Laura Henrietta died in 1830. Her sister Emma moved to Calcutta, where she was a journalist and newspaper editor, work she later continued in London. Her *Scenes and Characteristics of Hindostan* (1835) remains a classic of travel literature; she's a keen observer of the strangeness and extravagance of colonial life: the white ants' greed for textiles and furnishings, the appalling murder of horses to meet the demand for leather, and the colonies' (and white ants') craving for books. *At the Cape of Good Hope, the beach is said sometimes to be literally strewed with novels; an occurrence which takes place upon the wreck of a ship freighted from the warehouses of Paternoster Row.* Emma Roberts died in Bombay in 1840. Soon after the death of Laura, in 1832 Macnaghten had married Susanne Ann Halford. He wrote a memoir of military campaigns and also worked as a journalist in Calcutta; in *The Englishman* in 1838 he lampooned Dwarkanath Tagore (grandfather of Rabindranath Tagore) for his *love of Claret*. Macnaghten died in Calcutta in 1845.

Travelling in August 1825 on the Company's ship *Rose* to London via the Cape of Good Hope were Mrs Donnithorne, Mrs Bampton, with servants and ayahs to look after Miss Eliza Emily Donnithorne (aged four), Master H. Swetenham (aged six), and the recently orphaned Miss Selina Shakespear. Her father had just died and was buried at sea; her mother had passed away the previous year, of fever. Selina would join her sisters Marianne and Charlotte, who were with their aunt Charlotte Ritchie in London, to be educated at Mrs Ludlam's school, and by a *little old Polish lady*, Mme Zialtzke, who was particular about deportment, teaching the girls *to bow gracefully to imaginary friends*.

In 1823 James Donnithorne had become Salt Agent at Bullooah and Chittagong. During the night of 31 May and 1 June 1825 a severe hurricane and flood devastated these districts and the papers reported that Donnithorne was commended by the government for his management of relief operations.

Later that year he was appointed Salt Agent and Collector at Hidgellee, and the following June, 1826, he became Superintendant of the Hidgellee Salt Chokies (customs stations), a job his family and friends urged him not to take. He kept it for about nine years, despite a pay cut and the area's difficult climate, notoriously fatal to the European constitution. This is where Eliza must have spent some of her childhood.

Kedgeree, Khijiri, Kijari, Khadjuri – spellings vary – on the west bank of the *uncertain Hughli* River (as Kipling described it), is now mostly salt marsh – with an old British cemetery – but it was once an important anchorage for large ships. A website for the Crommelin family describes how a previous Salt Agent and Collector of Revenue at Hidgellee, Charles Russell Crommelin (1763–1822), ended his days in his house at Contai, *where he looks out for the arrival and departure of the East Indiamen anchored near the mouth of the Hoogly, usually at Kedgeree*. When he suffered a heart attack, his family rushed to his side, but they arrived too late. One of his descendants has told me that Contai at that time *was a lonely place with just a few neighbours* and those who lived there *travelled to and fro to Calcutta on the Hoogley*. In the salt agency, within a couple of years, Mr Crommelin was succeeded by Mr Plowden who was succeeded by Mr Reid, then Mr Manning, then Mr Donnithorne…Plowden, Reid and Manning (and possibly Crommelin too) all died of *Contai fever*: cholera. James was also sick, but recovered.

Perhaps he had moved into the Crommelin house. Ravaged by cyclones and floods, it's a tidal river region of alluvial plains where rice, bananas, mangoes and coconuts grow well, of sand dunes now planted with casuarina trees and keya bushes to stop erosion, and lagoons and salt marshes and expanses of dense swampy forest – the Sundarbans – home to an extraordinary range of wildlife. I wonder if as a child Eliza had heard the roar of Bengal tigers, if she knew the rose-like scent of the local kewra flowers – *Pandanus odoratissimus* – and retained an image in her mind of clay pots lined up for their distillation as perfume.

The Donnithornes' son William returned from England on the *Reliance* in 1828 and was appointed to the Bengal Civil Service. By 1829 William was Assistant to the Magistrate and Collector of Land Revenue at Allyghyr, by 1832 he was officiating Joint Magistrate and Deputy Collector of Agra.

James' family was often away, in England or at the Cape. In October 1831, the local press reported the arrival on the *Thomas Granville* of Mrs Donnithorne, *proceeding to her husband in Bengal*, accompanied by her daughters Penelope, Catherine Maria and Eliza (now aged 10), as well as servants M. A. Thomason and Betsy.

Calcutta markets were abundant with pineapples, melons, mangoes, oranges, guavas, loquats, strawberries and peaches. In a memoir, one taster of local fare, Mrs Meer Hasan Ali, made special mention of *a flat peach, with a small round kernel…the flavour of which is delicious, and the tree prolific*. Yams, Dutch beans, pumpkins and papayas were often reported as *plentiful*, and plantains *in perfection*. But you had to take care. Cholera is transmitted through contaminated food or water. It causes extreme diarrhoea and a person can die from dehydration within hours or a few days. The pulse races, eyes sink, skin turns a metallic blue. The disease was endemic to the Lower Ganges. Between 1817 and 1824, a cholera pandemic had spread from Bengal to other parts of India, then China, Japan and Indonesia, the Middle East and Russia; millions of people died. Second and third pandemics between 1827 and 1856 reached further, with outbreaks in Hungary, Germany, France, Britain, Egypt, and north and south America. Four more pandemics followed. Nineteenth-century scientists suggested a number of origins: high on the list were the swamps of Bengal and stagnant wells in the Kedjeree area. The quality of food and water on ships in warm climates was also under suspicion. The colonising forces of war, trade and an increase in global migration, carried the disease beyond its regional confinement. Common treatment with purgatives, or blistering, severely undermined a patient's chances of recovery.

Eliza's world was shattered in 1832 when at the age of eleven she lost her sisters in the Calcutta cholera outbreak. Sixteen-year-old Catherine Maria died on 11 June at Contai; eighteen-year-old Penelope died two days later, at Kedjeree. Soon after, Eliza also lost her mother. The Bengal Obituary reported the girls' deaths, and *the death of their fond mother, Sarah Eliza Donnithorne, the beloved and exemplary wife of James Donnithorne, Esq. of the Bengal Civil Service, who died of a broken heart at the Presidency, on the 4th day of September 1832, in the forty-fifth year of her age*. Recent studies show that grief can weaken the body's immune system, and – what we've always known instinctively – you can indeed die of a broken heart. Perhaps Eliza was spared because she was staying somewhere else with relatives, the Swetenhams, or Bamptons. But her bereavement at that young age must have left its mark.

In 1833 the pink and blue house in which the Donnithornes had lived at Fatehgarh became a cholera hospital.

Eliza's brother Edward moved to England and in 1834 married Elizabeth Jane Moore. Born 1809, she was the daughter of Rev. George Moore and Catherine Donnithorne, who was James Donnithorne's older sister; therefore Edward and his wife Elizabeth were first cousins. Consanguineous marriages were not uncommon at that time. Elizabeth's grandfather was Archdeacon of Cornwall and Canon of Exeter.

In Contai a hurricane in May 1833 almost destroyed James Donnithorne's house: doors and windows were shattered, rooms unroofed, large trees blown down, and the salt stores were destroyed; everyone feared the storm would break the embankments and cause widespread flooding. Donnithorne later reported *the extreme insalubrity of the Hidgellee district after the inundation of salt water*, and says *a more painful and harassing duty than* [my] *tour of inspection never devolved upon mortal, and my heart sickens at the recital of the vicissitudes to which I was exposed.*

His first-born son Lieutenant Henry Donnithorne, aged 35, died at the Calcutta Presidency in August 1834. In April 1835, his son William became a judge at Agra, the following year Officiating Joint-Magistrate and Sub-Collector of Etawah, and in 1837 Officiating Magistrate and Collector of Banda.

I'm uncertain about the exact chronology of James Donnithorne's appointments during his last years in India. It seems he continued as Officiating Salt Agent, Hidgellee until 1834, was subject to an inquiry into mismanagement involving fraud, theft and contraband of salt committed not by him but by officials in his charge, and was found to be *deficient in energy and active vigilance*. Despite putting up a fight in his own defence, he was dismissed from his post and from 1834–37 became Collector of Calcutta and the 24-Pergunnahs (the surrounding districts). The case is covered in an intense exchange of letters and documents published in *An Appendix to the Report from the Select Committee on Salt, British India, 1836*. The events must have taken their toll, because in July 1836 he was granted furlough *to sea, for one year, for health.*

Donnithorne was a member of the Australian Association of Bengal, which encouraged trade with Australia and settlement here after retirement in India. He was already in Sydney in 1836. In January that year he travelled on the *Eldon* from Sydney to Melbourne or Hobart. And he was certainly in Sydney in April, as his name appears on a guest list for the Festival of St George, held at the Pulteney Hotel on 22 April.

He was one of the Sons of Old England – about one hundred of them – commemorating the anniversary (on the 23rd) of their Patron Saint, with good wines, sirloin and pudding, toasts to King, Queen and Saint, music, speeches, wild applause and laughter. Donnithorne proposed Prosperity to the Country and *this toast was drunk with deafening cheers*. Alexander McLeay toasted the Ladies of the Colony, with a silly speech about being asked to do this because he was an old man and old men resembled old women. They drank to the judges and the clergy and to a rollcall of other saints and to each other and between each toast they sang an Air. It was reported that people went home wearing each other's coats and hats.

In August 1836 Donnithorne formed a pastoral partnership with Charles Hotson Ebden as manager. They started with Bonegilla Station on the Murray River near Albury, and a year later acquired Carlsruhe Station on the Campaspe. The following year James was in Adelaide; he had brought three horses to that town.

Sydney was no longer merely *the immense sink* into which the British poured their criminality. The Austrian naturalist Baron Charles von Hügel, visiting in 1834, thought *the inlet on which Sydney is situated appears to have been created by some mighty cataclysm of Nature*. He was less enchanted by *buildings stacked up one behind the other in the greatest disorder* creating *a confused townscape*, amazed that the Governor never bothered *to lay the town out on a more regular plan*. He noted it was a wealthy place, noted also the ubiquity of the Macquarie family, the drunks in George Street, and in the Botanical Gardens *everything lumped together... without rhyme or reason and without the slightest attention to scientific or aesthetic arrangement*. He admired the women. And the crop of pawpaws, guavas and *plants from India* in Alexander Macleay's garden at Elizabeth Bay. On the whole he found Sydney *detestable* and declared life in New South Wales *a cure for weak nerves*. But the longer he stayed, the more he liked it and finally he was sad to leave.

Another visitor that year, G. F. Davidson, remarked that the scenery was magnificent, hills and dales, windmills, and neat cottages perched on rock cliffs, glistening waters, *a picture that can scarcely be surpassed*; with one proviso, the green of the trees is *not quite brilliant enough*. What struck him most was the thorough Englishness of the place. He thought the greatest blight was the large number of public houses and consequently, the abundance of drunks.

In Sydney in 1836, Charles Darwin was impressed by its thriving commercialism, then shocked by its alcohol-fuelled ribaldry and *open profligacy*. He observed the bookshops were very small and their shelves very empty; it was not a place he'd choose to live in. Like von Hügel, Darwin was happiest travelling beyond the town.

The historian Isadore Brodsky has described Sydney's early years as a time when books were *circulating, borrowed, perhaps stolen*, and on the whole quite rare. A few people built up private libraries. And so we might imagine those who acquired the latest publications, only *six months behind the rest of the world*, immersed in Dickens' *Pickwick Papers*, Ralph Waldo Emerson's *Nature* or Arthur Schopenhauer's *On the Will in Nature*. A guidebook of the 1830s advises convicts to read only what is *calculated to improve your moral and religious welfare*.

Donnithorne lived in O'Connell Street, in the centre of town. If Eliza had accompanied her father, as has sometimes been assumed, then as a privileged young lady in Sydney, she may have spent the colder months in front of a fireplace with a book on her lap. Smouldering, let's say, under the influence of Byron's *Don Juan*. Perhaps she kept a diary. Most likely, she corresponded with her relatives in India and England. The winter of 1836 was very cold and mid-morning on 28 June, looking up from her reading, she would have been as astonished as everyone else to see light snow fall, enough to cover the hills down to the harbour. Newspapers reported that *the terrified state of the natives indicated the rare nature of such a visitation*. It has never snowed in Sydney again. And it's not known where Eliza spent the years after her sisters' and mother's deaths. Instead of coming to Australia with her father in the 1830s, it's possible that she was sent to England, perhaps as early as 1833.

In April 1837 Donnithorne returned to India on the *Royal George*. In March 1838 his son William was given leave of absence from his job as Officiating Joint-Magistrate and Deputy Collector of Allyghyr. He was to proceed to the hills for twelve months, to regain his health, and in

1839 he became joint Magistrate and Collector of Muzaffarnagar, north of Delhi, a fertile region known as the *sugar bowl* of India.

The *Sydney Herald* of 14 June 1838 noted that the *Emerald Isle* had sailed from Calcutta on 26 February. It was bringing settlers and capital, and passengers included Captain and Mrs Chisholm, and James Donnithorne, Esq. The Chisholms were ex-East India Company Captain Archibald Chisholm and his wife Caroline, now remembered as a philanthropist and one of Australia's great social reformers; she was a friend of Charles Dickens. The ship called at Madras, Swan River, King George's Sound, Port Adelaide, Hobart Town and Launceston, and reached Sydney on 20 August 1838. Donnithorne was bringing 15 bags of sugar, 757 bags of rice, 21 cases of wine, 4 hogsheads of beer, 12 boxes of candles, 4 cases of crockery, 1 trunk of books, 17 packages of bedding, a carriage, and 3 cases of brandy. He had been permitted to resign the British East India Company's Service and by the end of 1838 was settling into life in Sydney; amongst his papers there's an account for the purchase of eggs and potatoes.

In Twickenham

If Eliza was sent to England, she would have lived with relatives, most likely her older cousin Miss Anna Sherson (1796–1869), whose mother Maria Donnithorne was another of James' sisters, or with the Dawes family, close friends from India. It's not known what kind of education she received, she may have had private tutors, or attended school. Later, in her mid-twenties, she was described as *accomplished*, conventionally this meant she could sing, or play an instrument, sketch and sew, and speak French. In adulthood she was characterised as an insatiable reader and a collector of books; we also know she played piano and harp. Both the Sherson and Dawes households were near Hyde Park in London; later Eliza always kept in touch with them.

It's likely that by 1838 Eliza, aged seventeen, was living with her brother Edward and his wife Elizabeth Jane. Their daughter Isabella Charlotte had been born in 1836, followed by Henrietta Maria (1837), Mary Penelope (1839), Edward George Moore (1842), and Arthur Bampton (1844). For a short time they lived at Ailsa Park Villas, Isleworth Road, in Twickenham, with the convivial Charles Dickens as neighbour during June and July of 1838. His biographer Claire Tomalin points out that he wanted to be out of town for the coronation of Queen Victoria on 28 June. Dickens was just finishing *Oliver Twist* and starting *Nicholas Nickleby*; among his many guests were his friend John Forster (who had ditched, or was ditched by the writer Letitia Landon), the young novelist William Makepeace Thackeray (Selina Shakespear's cousin), and conversationalist Douglas Jerrold; George Henry Lewes was among his correspondents. Even if just to say 'good morning', Dickens must have known the Donnithornes and may have met Eliza; if she was looking after her niece Isabella, about the same age as Dickens' son Charley, they could have been invited to participate in the pony rides and balloon games Dickens liked to organise.

The Census of 1841 has the family, including Eliza, living at Colne Lodge on Hanworth Road (now Staines Road), Twickenham. Also listed was Edward Donnithorne, Elizabeth Donnithorne, their children Isabella, Henrietta and Mary, and four servants. Eliza's age is given as fifteen, in fact she was nineteen, turning twenty.

Colne Lodge was an impressive property, a large Palladian-inspired villa built about 1765; a plan (from a later period) shows landscaped and kitchen gardens, tennis lawn, stables and a paddock. And the house had had a succession of illustrious residents.

From 1767 to 1774 it was home to poet Paul Whitehead, of whom his earliest biographer Edward Thompson wrote that as a child *no sooner had he learnt to write, than all his letters and requests to his Father and Family were dressed in rhime*, and that later, choosing *to be a humble Imitator of one universally famous, [rather] than a small Original without weight to attract the attention of the the world*, he developed a *strong imitation* of Alexander Pope. Whitehead was a member of the Beef-Steak Club and more infamously, the Hell-Fire Club, a secret society led by Sir Francis Dashwood, later known as Baron Le Despencer, which was rumoured to have met in caves deep under West Wycombe Hill, where members indulged in esoteric underground mischief, and at nearby Medmenham Abbey, where the gardens and interior design are said to have been erotically themed. Thompson wrote, *Among other amusements, they had sometimes a mock celebration of the more ridiculous rites of the foreign Religious Order of the Church of Rome*. Other amusements involved women, fancy dress, rituals, and excessive food and alcohol. Horace Walpole called them *hermits*, to me they seem extremely sociable. The club motto was the Rabelaisian *Fais ce que tu voudrais*, inscribed over the doorway of the abbey. It's said that Whitehead knew too many secrets of too many powerful people, and a few days before his death, possibly suicide, he burnt all his papers in a great bonfire in the garden at Colne Lodge. He asked for his heart to be deposited in an elegant marble urn which was taken, with military pomp and a choir, to the mausoleum of his patron Lord Le Despencer.

From 1775 Colne Lodge was owned by the Countess of Dunmore. Her husband was the last royal governor of the Colony of Virginia, which he fled that year. It's rumoured that one of their daughters, Lady Augusta Murray, often received visits from Prince Augustus Frederick, son of George III, at Colne Lodge; Augusta and Augustus had married secretly in 1793 (a daughter was born 1794, a son 1801). Her youngest sister Lady Virginia Murray, born in Virginia in 1774, is known for trying to make a legal claim against the State of Virginia, to the effect that because they shared a name, she considered herself adopted by that State and it owed her an inheritance; the claim was not successful. This family didn't live at Colne Lodge for very long.

In 1776 it was leased to Captain John Tollemache, descended from the Tollemaches of nearby Ham House, and his wife Lady Bridget; he died defending his wife's honour in a duel in New York. His relative, the artist and feminist Mrs Delaney, commented to her grand-niece Mrs Port, *What a shocking end our worthless Cousin Tolmache has come to! kill'd (in America) in a duel by Mr Pennington, as worthless, I suppose, as himself. The cause of the quarrel, a song... What a furious animal is man without principles to check him, when he gives way to the violent sallies of his passions*; she reckoned that Lady Bridget was better off without him.

In 1786, during the residency of Benjamin Bradbury, the nurseryman and artist John Spyers produced an aquatint of Colne Lodge, presumably because he had designed its grounds, including the ornamental lake seen in the foreground of the picture. Previously Spyers had worked on Horace Walpole's garden at nearby Strawberry Hill and had helped Lancelot 'Capability' Brown with landscaping at Hampton Court.

It's supposed that for a short time in 1788 Robert Berry lived there with his daughters Mary and Agnes and that they were visited quite frequently by Horace Walpole, who was so enamoured with the sisters that he did his utmost to persuade them to settle in the neighbourhood.

With the result that they eventually moved into and inherited his house at Little Strawberry Hill. Next, Colne Lodge provided a roof over the heads of distinguished soldier and diplomat Lord William Shaw Cathcart and his family. Then it housed the Hon. Willbraham Tollemache, brother of the *worthless* John.

According to a Twickenham Museum webpage – titled Houses of Local Interest & their Occupiers – in 1816 Mrs Elizabeth Eardley Wilmot moved in. Or did she? She was the first wife of Sir John Eardley Eardley-Wilmot, who later became Lieutenant Governor of Van Diemen's Land. In their ten years of marriage they had eight children. And with these snippets of information I'm already imagining that it must have been a lively household at Colne Lodge before she died in 1818. I had ignored the museum's webpage disclaimer that *this is an incomplete survey, subject to ongoing correction and addition… [and that] dates may not indicate arrival or departure of an occupier… [and] exact dates have not yet been ascertained.* Historian Leonie Mickleborough, an expert on Eardley-Wilmot, tells me the family lived at Berkswell in Warwickshire, and that Elizabeth died after giving birth to her seventh and eighth children, twins, who were baptised at Berkswell. This reminds me again of the slipperiness of historical facts. I tone down my fantasy of the Eardley-Wilmots' high times with eight young children at Colne Lodge and shift to the possibility that they might have rented the house for a summer or two.

In any case, if lives leave a palimpsest in houses, Colne Lodge was a richly layered site, and it still had more to accrue.

1818 was the year Lady Virginia Murray inherited the villa from her mother. A later tenant was Lord Clifden. And in 1841 Lady Virginia, who lived in London and Paris, sold it to the Donnithornes.

I know very little about Eliza's life in Twickenham, but like her childhood home in Contai, it must have held for her many *dimensions of intimacy* (to borrow a phrase from the philosopher of dwellings, Gaston Bachelard). She would have walked around the riverside church of St Mary the Virgin where Alexander Pope is buried, and known his work. With her family she would have attended the newly built Holy Trinity Church on Twickenham Green, which I'm told her brother Edward helped finance and where in 1841 the first incumbent was his brother-in-law, Rev. Thomas Bevan (who had married Edward's wife's sister Mary Catherine Moore). I imagine that Eliza was as familiar with the meadowy lanes, narrow village streets and curves and islands of the Thames, as with the well-worn stories of love and intrigue associated with local sites, Marble Hill on one side of the river, Ham House on the other, the outline of Hampton Court Palace etched on the horizon, and new gossip emanating from the affairs of a succession of Waldegraves, who now owned Walpole's Gothic fancy, Strawberry Hill, only a short walk from Colne Lodge. When the vengeful 7th Earl Waldegrave, who was gaoled for riotous behaviour and blamed the Twickenham Bench for this injustice, decided to let Strawberry Hill go to ruin and rid himself of the cultural burden of its contents, he organised the Great Sale, which ran from the end of April to the end of June 1842. Thousands came to gawk, or to secure a rarity. The Donnithornes must have been among the crowd.

I see Eliza taking up her copy of Walpole's novel *The Castle of Otranto*; and I see her skimming the spines of other well-read Gothic novels on her bookshelves, in Twickenham and later in Australia.

In Australia

Now in his sixties, James Donnithorne had started a new life in Australia.

This is how another visitor, the explorer and scientist Paul Edmond de Strzelecki, saw us in 1839: I *have found…[at]…night in the streets of Sydney…the feeling of perfect security, and the delicious freshness of the air, mingled with nothing that could break the charm of a solitary walk…*adding that he couldn't believe this was reputedly *the most demoralised colony in the history of nations.*

Donnithorne was restless. In September 1839 he went from Sydney to Port Phillip on the *Pyramus*. His partnership with Ebden was dissolved; Ebden kept Bonegilla and Carlsruhe stations, James kept land and assets in the Kyneton district near Mount Macedon, where there's now a Donnithorne Street named after him. This property he called St Agnes. His manager was William Ward. Four months later, he returned to Sydney on the *Bright Planet* with his friends Ebden and Stuart Alexander Donaldson. He acquired other properties north of Melbourne, including Montmorency in Eltham, bought from Donaldson.

In Sydney he owned a family share in Roddam Farm at Watsons Bay on land that extended from present-day Camp Cove to Robertson Park; it was originally purchased for £71 by his father-in-law William Wright Bampton in 1795. As Judge Donnithorne, he moved in established circles that included Bishop Broughton and his family, the Governor of NSW Sir George Gipps, Donaldson (later the first Premier of NSW), and was close friends with the NSW Collector of Customs, John George Nathaniel Gibbes.

Gibbes was probably an illegitimate son of Prince Frederick, the second eldest son of King George III; he served in the Napoleonic wars, married and briefly had a bigamist marriage with another woman, became Collector of Customs in Jamaica, then in Great Yarmouth in East Anglia, and came to Australia in 1834; here he was a member of the NSW Legislative Council and Collector of Customs for the Colony. He introduced gaslighting to the streets of Sydney. As a young man in the late 1830s, Thomas Alexander Browne (later the novelist Rolf Boldrewood) was a school friend of the Gibbes' sons Edmund and Gussie (Augustus) and often visited them at their Palladian villa at Point

Piper; he was enchanted by the entire family: the *kindest hostess*, the *nicest girls*, there was a magnificent garden, fishing, boating, books, music, late dinners. The family lived in a number of grand houses, including Wotonga, which Gibbes built at Kirribilli Point – they moved there in 1843 – with sweeping views of Sydney harbour, now part of Admiralty House. He retired in 1859, when one of his sons, William John Gibbes, a bit of a rogue, was involved in a smuggling scandal, and moved to Yarralumla, now the official residence in Canberra of the Governor-General of Australia.

Another friend, and also James' physician, was Dr William Bland. A pardoned convict who'd killed a man in a duel in India, Bland was also a satirist and politician, with strong democratic instincts; he especially liked to target Governor Macquarie. He fought against religious fanaticism, was a founder of Sydney College, and the first president of the Australian Medical Association. As a doctor it's said he was skilful and kind. Called *the poor man's friend*, he often refused payment for medical advice or treatment; interested in homeopathy, he specialised in snake bite cures. Bland was also Caroline Chisholm's physician and a great supporter of her projects. At the back of his house in Pitt Street he grew violets, roses, rock lilies, aquatic plants, vines, loquat and peach and fig trees, pineapples, strawberries, rare currants, gooseberries, dates and bananas, jasmine, passionfruit, geraniums, honeysuckle, hydrangeas, wallflowers, myrtles, lavenders, larkspurs, pinks, sunflowers, and snowdrops. Walk down Pitt Street now and imagine that! It's likely when they got together, Bland and Donnithorne talked horticulture. The doctor owned a country retreat at Prospect Creek (now Carramar), where an oak he planted still stands. He invented – among other things – an *atmotic ship*, an airship that would cut down travel time between Australia and Britain to 4–5 days. The earliest known daguerrotype portrait taken in Australia, by George Goodman in 1845, was of Dr William Bland. A half-blind magpie, a very small lapdog and a cockatoo who said *Dr Bland's pretty boy*, were his pets.

Like his friend, James Donnithorne also had a strong sense of public duty. He belonged to the Superintending Committee of the Benevolent Society that raised funds for settlers in need, subscribed to John Gould's publication of *The Birds of Australia*, and may have been involved in planning or fundraising for Leichhardt's 1844 expedition to Port Essington. He was renowned for his *unbounded hospitality* and it's been said that *as his wealth increased so did his generosity*. But while he was respected and revered, he was also *feared as a man not to be trifled with*.

In January 1840 Donnithorne, retaining primary ownership of his property St Agnes, entered into a business partnership with the manager William Ward. The signing of the agreement in Melbourne was witnessed by Stuart Alexander Donaldson, with whom he also co-owned sheep and land in the New England district. On 13 January

1840 Donnithorne, Donaldson and Ebden again made the trip back to Sydney together. He'd left a number of people to work at St Agnes. Ward set out to improve the property, and another they had acquired north of Castlemaine at Mount Alexander; but he ran into debt, the economy was in depression, and Mount Alexander and part of St Agnes had to be sold. The consequences of Ward's mismanagement caused everyone involved great anguish.

In Sydney Donnithorne was one of the first members of the Australian Club. He lived in Fort Street, and had another home in Cumberland Street, which commanded *a full view of the Town and Harbour*; his neighbours included the artist Conrad Martens, and Dr James Mitchell, whose son David Scott Mitchell grew up to be a book collector, library benefactor, and some say, a recluse. In May 1841 the *Sydney Morning Herald* reported that at the Cumberland Street residence, *Messrs 'Lemon Syrup' (his Honour's Bengalee cook), and William Jones (his Honour's footman), had a quarrel when in their cups, and although Jones, by his superior pugilism, was the conqueror, yet Mr Lemon Syrup managed to give his antagonist a passable memorial of the contest in the form of a black eye*. The reason: Mr Syrup accused Mr Jones of stealing from the larder. Police were called, they searched the premises for evidence, nothing was found, Jones was nonetheless taken into custody, brought before a judge, and discharged. In June Donnithorne and Donaldson departed Sydney on the *Sea Horse* for Port Phillip; Donnithorne returned to Sydney on the *Isabella Watson* in September, with three servants. In November he was part of a deputation that presented Alexander McLeay with *a very handsome silver Candelabrum*. James Donnithorne had been living with Ann Kelly. She was born in 1817 on the ship which brought her parents to Australia and about 1835, aged 18, she had married James Davidson; they had three daughters. It's possible that Donnithorne had met Ann – their age difference was 44 years – at his property near Kyneton; or that she went there with him; their son James Kelly was born in Victoria (presumably at St Agnes Station) on 11 October 1841. The child was baptised a month later, on 14 November 1841, at St Phillip's Church in Sydney, as the son of James and Ann *Donthorn*, the father's profession is given as *farmer*.

In India that year his son William Sherson Donnithorne, aged thirty four, married a widow, Sophia Emmeline Josephine Smith (née Patton). They had two sons who died young and Sophia died in 1844.

Donnithorne advertised his Cumberland Street house for rent in January 1843, followed in February by the sale of his *costly and very elegant surplus Furniture and Effects*, which was held on the premises. It offered *splendid* candleholders, *handsome* Delph vases, Dresden china ornaments, a chest of plate, French clocks, linen, a couple of four-post mahogany bedsteads, mirrors, marble washstands, fishing equipment, dining and library tables: the property of a man of *superior judgement in all matters of taste*.

By April Donnithorne is back at St Agnes, where purchases by Miss Kelly include rose oil, honey, a pot of Naples soap, saffron, and medicines Bot. Rhubarb and Magnesium, refinements one doesn't associate with farm life in the Australian bush at that time. Admitted to the Melbourne Club in October 1843, he remained a member for two years. The club recorded details of his family background and career, described him as a civil officer and pastoralist, and noted he'd *brought to NSW a large amount of capital.*

He was trying to sell subdivisions of Roddam Farm, but withdrew the sale. In January 1844, the *Sydney Morning Herald* advertised *TO BE LET, furnished, for a long or short period, the house lately occupied by Mr Donnithorne in Fort-street…Enquire at the Custom House.* In February Donnithorne's servant Samuel Jones was selling *one or two ALLOTMENTS…two miles from Sydney*, and for a free passage he was offering his services to any family returning to England.

Back again at St Agnes, James' household accounts reveal a need for acetic acid, camphorated chalk, a dozen packets of rhubarb and magnesium, 2 oz of isinglass, peppermint, laudanum, refined liquorice, and exhibit a taste for good clothes, ale and brandy, Windsor soap and other luxuries. In July he shopped in Melbourne at D&S Benjamin, purchasing a mohair coat. In September a court case began to sort out the problems of mismanagement at St Agnes station. The problem was alcohol: the sly grog industry in the Mount Macedon region was increasing. I've read that one trick was to sell someone a bottle of pickles and give them a free bottle of rum. It was discovered that Ward was a frequenter of taverns and pubs; he was paying for his bottles of port with sheep and other farm goods; he gambled and got into fights at Melbourne's racecourse. In November 1844 Donnithorne returned to Sydney on the steamer *Shamrock*; his favourite beverages on board were tea, wine, brandy and ale. He had not been a successful squatter.

Court hearings in the case of *Donnithorne v Ward* finished in June 1845. The judge said *persons who had sheep on the basis upon which Ward had them were, in no way, partners in the undertaking. Their position was that of persons who went on an adventure for a share of the profits such as sailors on a whaling cruise*; he ruled the agreement to be terminated, but the case was still unsettled at the end of 1845 and Donnithorne was disillusioned. His accounts show he'd bought muriatic acid and a stopper bottle, bismuth, alum, sulphuric acid, best Russian isinglass, a sponge, and camphor liniment. They point to eye trouble, chest cold, an upset stomach, and unless the isinglass was required for blancmange, Donnithorne too was brewing his own beer. He bought a number of household items from Edward Salamon at an auction, including a parrot cage. Three years later a letter in *The Argus* reported William Ward's *melancholy death* from *the ruinous tendency of an immoderate use of intoxicating liquors.*

On 26 April 1845 Eliza's uncle William Wright Bampton, son of the Captain, had died at Colne Lodge in Twickenham. A gravestone inscription at Oak Lane Cemetery reads, *In memory of Major William Bampton. Late of the 70th Regiment who had served with that Corps upwards of 20 years during which period he was often engaged with the enemy…received a dangerous wound at the battle of Dieg in Hindostan, was present at the siege of Flushing and the retreat of Corunna.*

One eyewitness report of the Battle of Dieg in 1804, in the Second Anglo-Maratha War in Central India, by Lt. Col. John Pester, describes an attack on the village of Aow. *Shot, stones and brick were flying at a tremendous rate, and many men of our regiment were killed and wounded by the two latter, as well as shot,* General Fraser *lost his leg by a shot. Many a gallant fellow fell also…*enemies *were spiked with our bayonets…the carnage among the enemy was such as on cool reflection would make the hardest heart relent… Poor Forbes, who fell in the village, we all lamented most sincerely…a cannon shot struck him to pieces…Seven officers killed, and nineteen wounded; of the latter, several died of their wounds.*

The Battle of Corunna, fought in Spain in January 1809, was the first major engagement between the British and French during the Napoleonic wars; counting the casualties on both sides, about 2,500 men died or were wounded.

The Siege of Flushing occurred in July and August the same year. Attempting to open another front against Napoleon, who was fighting Austria, a British force of over 300 ships and 40,000 men reached the

Dutch island of Walcheren where a French garrison was stationed at Flushing. A veteran of that battle, with a taste for the slapstick of war – or perhaps just a realist – has told how the *French understood irregular firing much better than our men*, and how on one occasion when officers sat down to eat a freshly cooked dinner, the cook was shot through the heart, the officers *made his narrow home, at the spot on which he had set our table…and dined over the old cook who had dressed our meal.* But then the British got stuck on the island, and morale faded over the next months, when over 4,000 men died there of so-called Walcheren Fever, a lethal mix of malaria, typhus and typhoid fever. Some estimates are as high as 8,000 dead and tens of thousands ill.

Aged 59 and an officer on half pay, William Bampton's death certificate says he was found dead at Colne Lodge: *Suicide by discharging the contents of a loaded pistol into his mouth – the state of his mind unknown.* He was buried by the Rev. Thomas Bevan.

Did Eliza hear the shot? Find the body? Whatever happened, in the words of one descendant, *he leaves a large amount of dosh just to her.* It must have been this event while she was living at Colne Lodge which levered Eliza out of England, and this inheritance which allowed her to travel to Australia.

Oddly, in the same week as Major Bampton's suicide, a one-year-old infant called William James Bampton, the son of Henry Bampton, a Twickenham gardener, also died. It appears to be a coincidence; a search has not turned up any connection between the families of the major and the gardener.

In Australia, Ann Kelly's daughter Anna was born in 1846 and baptised at Saint Phillip's Church on 4 January 1846; her parents were named as William and Ann Kelly. To confuse us further, Ann then married Samuel Jones in April 1847 at St Andrew's Church in Sydney. The child was probably James Donnithorne's. There was even speculation among descendants that she might have been Eliza's, but of course Eliza didn't arrive in Sydney until later that year.

James was now living in Sydney, on the North Shore, perhaps near his friend Gibbes, who had recently moved to the harbour front at Kirribilli. His household purchases show a parasol, ribbon, wool, dress, cups and saucers; in May 1846 he bought sixteen yards of satin from Joseph Farmer, in June hats from John Thomas, in July the Overture to Henry IV. The Donnithornes were a musical family, and Eliza would soon arrive with her pianoforte and her harp. In November James bought a pair of lady's cloth boots and a pair of boy's boots, and similar purchases continued into 1847. Some of these items might have been for Eliza, but it seems that despite Ann's marriage (maybe one of convenience), James continued to care for her and her children.

It's possible that by this time Eliza had already had a romantic attachment, or had made up her mind to remain single. Probably she was deeply affected by the death of her uncle. Some say twenty-five is the age an unmarried woman becomes a spinster. Eliza Donnithorne, not quite twenty-five, left London on 8 March 1846 – *a summer-like Sunday* – and travelled to Sydney for nearly four months on board the *Agincourt*, arriving at Port Jackson 25 June 1846. It was regarded by a fellow passenger, Col. Godfrey Charles Mundy – sketcher, soldier, author – as *a shipful of strangers bound to a strange land*. He really wasn't sure about this adventure, he thought *a Man must be leading in Europe a very sad, solitary, or unsatisfactory existence, who can, without many a pang of regret, many a sigh of painful separation, gird up his loins, shoulder his wallet, and clutch his staff, for a pilgrimage to Australia*. But the food on board was good, a cow provided fresh milk, along the way one could learn about marine ornithology, and for readers, *everyone throws his small store of books into the common stock*. Despite his scepticism, he was excited to enter the Heads…*grand and appropriate portal of one of the noblest harbours in the world*. Then disappointed again, by *the leaden tint of the gum-tree foliage, and…the dry and sterile sandstone from which it springs*.

Setting foot in Sydney, Mundy thinks it's *more exclusively English in its population than either Liverpool or London. Were it not for an occasional orange-tree in full bloom…or a flock of little green parrots…one might fancy himself at Brighton or Plymouth*. He was more convinced of his whereabouts when he was invited to dine, on wallaby tail soup, kangaroo haunch, wonga-wonga pigeon with bread sauce, and exotic fruit for dessert. He was not impressed with the town's lighting, paving or sewerage, nor the large number of ownerless dogs and stray goats.

I wonder if Eliza shared his views; I think parrots – all the birds here, swaggering cockatoos and clownish pink corellas, brush turkeys, magpies, currawongs and melodious butcher birds, tiny wrens in low bushes, honeyeaters, wattlebirds, the kookaburra and black swan – they would have delighted her.

The Governor Sir George Gipps' departure ceremony was held with much pomp on 15 July 1846, attended by the bulk of Sydney society, including James Donnithorne, and perhaps also his daughter. In June 1847 *Bell's Life in Sydney and Sporting Reviewer* (which would later become the *Australasian Post*) reported that one evening the *learned gentleman* Judge Donnithorne was *proceeding along Macquarie Street towards the Circular Wharf, to embark for the North Shore*, when he was knocked down by two *ruffians*, one held his hand over the Judge's mouth, the other went through his pockets. I'm assuming the Donnithornes lived on the North Shore until about 1848.

Then they moved into Camperdown Lodge, which stood on a ridge on the southern side of the harbour, with views to Botany Bay. This house was part of an estate on Cooks River Road, owned by John Icke Kettle, a magistrate who had bought the land from the descendants of William Bligh who had been granted it by Governor King in 1806. The area was named by Bligh for a British naval victory over the Dutch in 1797, which had occurred in the North Sea near the village of Camperduin. Camperdown Lodge stood in adjacent Newtown.

This land was once native forest and grasslands, maintained by the Gadigal band of the Eora people for hunting kangaroos. They fished along the Cooks River. After invasion, many died during the smallpox epidemic of 1789, but survivors continued to live in the Newtown area and other parts of Sydney. Land grants further destroyed their ancient traditions. Their bush track between Port Jackson and Botany Bay – part of a coastal network of trading routes – was widened by settlers to become a major thoroughfare known as the Bulanaming Road, later Cooks River Road, now King Street. A community of settlers grew up around Webster's New Town Store on the corner of Cooks River Road and Eliza Street. In one account, in the late 1830s the population of the district consisted of *877 Protestants, 364 Roman Catholics, one Pagan, one Jew*. In the 1840s it was described as *a beautiful village* and the stream under Newtown Bridge still had good drinking water.

It's been suggested to me by historian John Johnson that Camperdown Lodge was probably built by John Kettle around 1844, and was first advertised for lease in April of that year. It's believed the first tenant c. 1844–1846 was Alderman Henry McDermott.

Camperdown Lodge was then leased by Edmund Minto Gibbes and Frances (Fanny) Simmons. She was the daughter of James Simmons, emancipist and active member of Sydney's Jewish community. Fanny and

Edmund had eloped the previous year. A member of the Gibbes family noted in September 1846 that *Eddy is missing again* and described it as *a rather notorious affair*. In August 1847 Fanny, aged about fifteen, gave birth at Camperdown Lodge; a few months later, the baby died there. The couple had another son, born at Donnithorne's property in Watsons Bay. Maybe as a friend of Gibbes, James made his house available to them when they required a refuge. Fanny and Edmund overcame family opposition and married, but their second child also died, and Edmund died soon after, at sea. It was a close family and his father would later bequeath one of his daughters a drawing of *the Ship in which my dear son Edmund sailed for England and died*. Fanny remarried.

We know the Donnithornes were living at Camperdown Lodge by 1849, because we know that in 1849 and 1851 two infants, Ann and Mary Isabella Larkman died there soon after birth: they were the daughters of Donnithorne's ex-convict butler and bodyguard Charles James Larkman and his wife Ann Sefferidge. Fond of the Larkmans, in his will the Judge left them a pension of £50. So close to home, some of these events just after Eliza's arrival must have disturbed her. Camperdown Lodge was a busy household, reflecting the colony's and particularly James Donnithorne's own conviviality. As for nurturing a Miss Havisham, it could just as easily have sheltered a Magwitch, Dickens' convict, who had been deported to New South Wales, where he became a wealthy pastoralist.

Because Dickens created a sense of contiguity between the zombie-like recluse Miss Havisham and the domestic armageddon of Satis House – the twinned morbidity of heart and hearth – and because reclusion is so often expressed spatially, in terms of a person's extreme and illogical attachment to her or his place of retreat, as in the case of the nineteenth-century American poet Emily Dickinson, who became chronically ensconced not just in her house but in one room, so it has always been assumed that Eliza owned Camperdown Lodge, that it was her special place. It's important to note, however, that first James, and then Eliza, never owned the house; they rented it from Kettle, who retained ownership until his death in 1881.

Kettle's daughter Mary had married Robert Brock in 1853. Camperdown Lodge was on the corner of King and Georgina Streets, named after Kettle's other daughter, Georgina Thruchly. The Brock and Thruchly families lived nearby and in the 1880s built a row of grand terraces, now 3–6 Warren Ball Avenue across from Hollis Park. In about 1883 Kettle's grandson George Brock, once a Newtown haberdasher, managed the estate and continued to lease it to Eliza until her death in 1886. When George came into his full inheritance, he built a French chateau at Mona Vale, known as Brock's Folly; he had big plans, went broke, and the Kettle Estate was wound up around 1905.

As subscribers to the St Andrew's Cathedral building fund in 1847, Mr and Miss Donnithorne appear near the top of a list headed by

Lieutenant-Colonel Gibbes. Edmund Blacket was the new cathedral's architect. Sometimes they entertained their friends. At all times they ate well. A bill on 20 June that year, from the Australian Grocery and Italian Provisions Warehouse, for several months of shopping, includes caviar, cheeses, oysters, bottled fruit, pickles, figs, pies and many fruit tarts; their butchers' bills are not reading matter for the faint-hearted. But not everyone was convinced of James' social standing: in November 1847, Roger Therry sailed with him on the *Agincourt* and writes a little snidely to Patrick Bonaventure Geoghegan that *Mr, commonly called Judge, Donnithorne*, is a fellow passenger.

In January 1848 Alexander Mollison, who held James Donnithorne's power of attorney, offered the remainder of St Agnes for private sale and in February 1848 it was advertised to be auctioned in April. It's described as *unsurpassed for its abundance of pasturage and water in all seasons*, the flock consisting of 18,000 sheep, *fine woolled* and *perfectly clean*. There's a cottage and garden, a wool shed, well-fenced paddocks, with two drays and twelve bullocks thrown in for good measure. It failed to reach an acceptable offer, but was eventually sold in late 1849.

Did James need the money for Eliza's wedding? On Saturday 8 April 1848 a gossip column in *Bell's Life in Sydney and Sporting Reviewer* announced, *'On Dit'* that *The member for Durham is about to lead to the hymeneal altar the accomplished daughter of Judge Donnithorne; rumour adds that the 'man of fashion' has eight thousand reasons for so doing.*

The member for Durham – an area north of the Hunter River, one of the original Nineteen Counties of NSW, where he was newly sworn in on 21 March 1848 – was none other than James' old friend and business partner Stuart Alexander Donaldson.

Donaldson, born in England in 1812, was a merchant and pastoralist. In his youth he travelled in Europe and Mexico. He was good friends with Strzelecki, who asked him before leaving on an expedition in December 1839 to dispose of his papers in the event of death, as he was off to climb Australia's highest mountain. Like Donnithorne, Donaldson belonged to the Australian Club. He was opposed to the transportation of convicts, was an elected member of the old Legislative Council and then of the NSW Legislative Assembly, and would serve one term as Premier – the first Premier of NSW (for less than three months) – and as Colonial Secretary (1856), Colonial Treasurer (1856–1859), and consul-general for Sardinia; he was knighted in 1860. It's been said (a comment made by Henrietta Heathorn, who would marry the biologist and Darwin's *bulldog* Thomas Henry Huxley) that Donaldson did not lack self-esteem. The naturalist John Gilbert thought him an *upstart* and a *coxcomb*. Famously, Donaldson criticised the Surveyor-General Sir Thomas Mitchell's over-expenditure, and was challenged to a duel, which they fought at dawn at the Water reserve, now Centennial Park, on 27 September 1851. Each fired three shots, and missed. Donaldson's hat was ruined. Their ornate set of French .50 calibre pistols with percussion locks and walnut butts is in the National Museum in Canberra.

I asked one of Donaldson's descendants – from the line of his son Lester Stuart whose mother was Mary Leicester – if she knew more. She replied, *We don't know if he was a man of fashion, nor is there any info about Eliza Donnithorne.* And *It seems Lester Stuart was born out of wedlock, but clearly was recognised (and presumably financially assisted) by his father.* Born in Sydney in 1841, Lester was educated in England and in 1858 returned to Australia, where he became a merchant, pastoralist, magistrate and amateur burlesque actor. Lester's father had also gone to England in 1841, and returned to Australia in 1844, when he found his businesses here were being mismanaged. So in 1848, when he was supposed to have been engaged to marry Eliza Donnithorne, his financial situation might still have been precarious – the reference in *Bell's Life* that he stood to gain financially from the attachment suggests this was the case – and he already had a mistress and a son. Perhaps Eliza knew this? Donaldson's prospects subsequently improved during the gold rush and in England in 1854 he married Amelia Cowper; they returned to Sydney in 1855. The writer Rachel Henning thought he was too stout, too bumptious, and that he ate too much. Perhaps Eliza thought so too. Or perhaps, as rumour has it, she had her eye on someone else.

If there was to have been a wedding, I thought the most likely church, based on James Donnithorne's friendship with Bishop Broughton and his circle, would have been St James' in King Street. But there is no record of a proposed union of Donnithorne and Donaldson in the marriage banns and applications for licences at St James' from 1848 to the 1850s, nor in the banns at Newtown's St Stephen's. Of course it's possible that the gossip column got it wrong, and Eliza was engaged to be married, but not to the Member for Durham.

Eavesdroppers 1: So What Happened?

For heaven's sake don't stop me if you've heard this plot before, because it's pennies for peanuts you have.
George Blaikie, 'Mr Cuthbertson shoots through', *Western Mail* (Perth)
4 February 1954

In Twickenham, Edward Donnithorne's wife Elizabeth Jane had died aged thirty-seven in March 1847; her youngest child was only three. It's not known what kind of relationship Eliza had with her cousin and sister-in-law Elizabeth. If they were close, this death would have been a sad reminder of her own losses in childhood, and another jolt so soon after the tragic death two years earlier at Colne Lodge of her uncle William Bampton. Edward remarried a few years later, became a magistrate and was active in local politics.

Within such an intensely familial and at times distressing atmosphere of births and deaths would Eliza have considered romance as an escape? Or would she have seen it as a liability? And would she have found opportunities for a clandestine courtship that led to wedding plans? Was she jilted? No one really knows what happened. Possibly her father – *a man not to be trifled with* – tried to arrange matches for her with men like Donaldson, and she rejected them. In an era when women of her class were expected to marry suitably, it's to her credit that she did not become a pawn in colonial dynastics.

It's said she met someone she loved, her father objected to their marriage but then gave in, and on the wedding day the groom did not turn up. From that moment on, in case he was delayed, Eliza is supposed to have suffered an extreme form of lovesickness, worn her wedding dress for the rest of her life and over four decades kept the wedding feast laid out. Psychiatric science now understands a person painfully obsessed with lost love and caught up in what's called *complicated or 'stuck' grief* as suffering from *Miss Havisham Effect*, a malformation of social attachment and a form of addiction.

Not only has no evidence of the intended wedding been found, there's also significant uncertainty about the date. One version has Eliza abandoned in 1846 (the year she arrived), other versions cite 1848, and even as late as 1856 (after her father's death). Apart from a name, an oddly specific detail – it's supposed to have been someone called

George Cuthbertson – there's no evidence of the identity of the groom. He's been cast as a naval or army officer, a shipping clerk, and if not exactly a villain, as a bit of a weakling. The electoral roll for Gipps Ward shows a George Cuthbertson living at 103 Clyde Street The Rocks in 1845. Who was he and was he the one? My hunch is, that jilted or not jilted, Eliza became a recluse and this fact was strange enough for the rest of the story in all its florid detail to grow around her.

We don't know what she looked like. If Eliza was ever drawn or painted, the artist might have been Charles Rodius (1802–1860), or William Nicholas (1809–1854). Nicholas portrayed poets, publicans and piemen, speculators, sportsmen, schoolmasters and soldiers, whisperers and women, and an inspector of public nuisances Mr T. Stubbs, as well as several members of the Gibbes family. Quirkily he sometimes hid his signature; in a portrait of Mary Murray (Gibbes) it was discovered recently inscribed in the pattern of an oriental carpet on which the subject stands. Not all his subjects have been identified. One day we might find a Portrait of an Unknown Woman – a watercolour, or lithograph – by Nicholas, or someone else, to be a likeness of Eliza. It seems too much to hope for a photograph of her.

I asked a great-great granddaughter of Eliza's brother Edward what she thought. She replied, *The Donnithornes seemed to have kept their Cornish Celtic looks. This being usually dark hair, frequently with grey or blue eyes and pale skin. But they were not a handsome family – many were tall and rather gangly. Stick thin…usually quite assertive, clever and the women were quite tough and spirited…There were no photos of Donnithorne blonde haired beauties!!*

When gold was found west of Sydney and late in 1851 fortune hunters headed to Ophir, Sofala, Wallaby Rocks, and Dutchman's Ridge, the *Empire* reported that *Old Dick Hurst, late in the employ of Mr Justice Donnithorne, of Newtown, has in three weeks netted £150 without much trouble, as but little top stuff has to be thrown off.*

James Donnithorne died 25 May 1852, aged 79. He was buried two days later in Camperdown Cemetery. The ceremony was performed by the Bishop of Sydney, William Grant Broughton. His executors were J.G.N. Gibbes, Dr. Bland, and Rev. Charles Campbell Kemp, the first Rector of Newtown's St Stephen's. Each received a mourning ring. Donnithorne left legacies for his servant Larkman, and to Ann Kelly Jones, who also received land at Kiama, and to her son James and daughter Anna. He left property in India, including Contai, to his son Edward. And an annuity to a servant of his late wife. The *Sydney Morning Herald* obituary for *The Late James Donnithorne, Esquire* (no mention of *Judge*) made much of the Donnithorne family's royal connections and his service in India, his *unbounded hospitality* and *universal benevolence* and said he retired to Australia because he preferred *the genial climate of this favoured land.*

Eliza inherited her father's substantial Australian estate, and spent the rest of her life managing her various incomes. With her brother Edward she co-owned Roddam Farm at Watsons Bay, which they sold in 1854. Half a century later, Christina Stead, aged 15, moved with her family to Pacific Street, Watsons Bay. It would become the fictional setting for her best-known novel, *The Man Who Loved Children*, which explores a child's experience of crowdedness and solitude inside her family. The female protagonist, Louie (a self-portrait) is made to feel like an outsider by her stepmother, but *it happened that this solitude was exactly what Louie most craved.* According to her biographer Hazel Rowley, Stead's grandfather was a keen Dickensian and she *liked to think her family history was shaped by literature*, but she was probably unaware that Boongarre, their house named after an Aboriginal chief who had lived in the area, where she'd spent *wonderful, solitary hours… describing things to herself*, stood on land once owned by the supposed model for Miss Havisham.

I consider facts and fictions and get caught up in far-fetched digressions. I discover that current biographical information about Eliza Donnithorne is often doubtful or peripheral, and that there's a scarcity of reliable early sources, nothing prior to her death in 1886. But talk was rife.

Amongst the Donnithorne material now at Sydney's Marrickville Library, there's a photocopy of a cutting with the handwritten reference

The Echo, 1888. It's an article about Newtown, and it describes *the cottage of Judge Donnithorne* and *the number of rumours afloat about it*. The author hedges, then goes on. *It is a private matter, and we have no right to inquire into particulars; but it has been so much talked of that a history of Newtown would not be complete without some reference to it.* The author speculates. *The most feasible story appears to be that, shortly after the death of the Judge, the house was occupied by a lady, and one day her brother or cousin left the place, vowing he would never return. The lady, it is said, asked him to come back, and told him that if he did he should never find the door shut against him. Whether this is the true version or not matters little.* What matters is that *the lady* made a vow and kept it literally, as *the front door was never closed*. There's also a description of the house, *which stood back from the road, and was almost hidden by four huge Norfolk Island pines and a tangle of sweetbriar and other shrubs*...with a tall fence in front. The *lady* was rarely seen and some thought the place was haunted. It was now boarded up, the pines cut down, the ground marked out for building lots.

Another of these first articles is titled 'Our Metropolitan Suburbs: Newtown' in the *Illustrated Sydney News* (1889). It mentions Cambridge Hall (as Camperdown Lodge had been renamed): old, one-storied, brick and stucco, and *not in the least ornamental*. And tells of the Judge and his daughter, and the jilting – *a bridegroom is indispensable on these interesting occasions* – and the mystery surrounding his sudden *evanishment*, and how it affected Eliza, who never left the house again. While I scoff at the embellishments of this story, there's one detail I like: the mention of Eliza's books. I feel it doesn't fit the stereotype, it's something those early mythmakers would not have made up, so it must be true. It's said *her habits became decidedly eccentric…her only solace being books. She became an insatiable reader, and when she died, less than two years ago, she left an extensive and valuable library behind her*. Notably, it's this *insatiable* reader and these books that are missing from Dickens' portrait of Miss Havisham and Satis House. The article also insists that Eliza was truly kind, that she had a *natural sweetness of disposition, and she is still borne in grateful remembrance at Newtown for her many acts of unobtrusive benevolence*. While she gave freely, and some people got to speak with her through a *nearly closed door*, she was *invariably invisible*.

Another article I consider is 'An Afternoon's Ramble over Historic Ground', by G.C.J. published in the *Hawkesbury Herald* of 20 November 1903. It describes a walk the author took through parts of Newtown, including a visit to St Stephen's Church – *How cool it was under that high Gothic roof* – in the company of William Freame, who (it claims) had lived in Newtown and attended the church as a boy and was now a student of Divinity. It offers the usual story about the jilted Eliza Donnithorne; but the name Freame is intriguing as it will crop up again.

On the internet I come across but find it impossible to purchase a novel called *Eliza* (All Romance Books, 2005) by John Godl, who is also the author of a number of articles about the Donnithornes. I try to contact him. Google locates him as curator of Sydney's Bus and Truck Museum, but my email is returned, and when I phone the museum the man who answers says *no, Godl doesn't work here any more.* I express disappointment and he says *hang on, I'm on my own here but I'll go and ask someone else.* Puts the phone down. Waiting for a long time for information about Godl I hear shuffling, clanking, a door, and a woman's voice announcing I *left my umbrella here yesterday!* with sounds receding as they go looking for the umbrella. I hang up, phone back later. Jim Carter says there's a lot going on, the museum's moving from Tempe to Leichhardt; he thinks at the new site there won't be much room for trucks, so eventually it'll just be buses, double-deckers, they're the favourites. Wistfully I say *yeah the old green and cream ones.* Godl, he tells me, looked after the museum's archives, but has *sort of departed the scene.* He says this twice, with emphasis, and I'm not sure what he means. He'll try and find him for me.

Meanwhile I've been in touch with Anthony Beckles Willson, who among other things has written on Alexander Pope's love of mastiffs and minerals and conducts tours of Pope's Grotto in Twickenham; I'd contacted him to ask if I could see the Grotto as I'd be in London in the summer. Beckles Willson says he knows Godl, whose article about the Donnithornes is published on the Twickenham Museum's website, and confirming he's definitely the one to contact, gives me his current email address. Godl answers many of my questions and generously sends me loads of material, including the manuscript of his novel. However, I sense he is anxious that the genealogical and general data he's been collecting for many years should confirm his own version of the Donnithorne family and of Eliza's life, which he insists is based on reliable research including personal interviews and the authority of local historians and journalists such as J.M. Forde, W.H.G. Freame, and Colbert Moore.

But I suspect these writers simply chased a good story, emptied Eliza Donnithorne's life of its humdrum and filled it with the fanciful transcriptions of an urban myth. Under the cosy pseudonym of Old Chum, Joseph Michael Forde wrote what one of his obituarists called *delightful gossip*, for the *Truth*, a Sydney paper generally regarded as a scandal sheet. In one Sunday edition of the *Truth* (18 May 1924), where Forde thanked friends for their good wishes on his 85th birthday, his page recounted Ben Boyd's Fate and The McIvor Robbery and featured a photo of Camperdown Lodge, *home of the late Miss Eliza E. Donnithorne, the eccentric daughter of an East Indian Judge*: it shows the pillared entrance of a house flanked by windows with shutters, on the right a tree, perhaps a frangipani, and a child sitting on the stone steps leading up to an open door.

An article in the *Sun Herald* in 1911, on houses with *romantic histories*, is almost identical to the earlier one in the *Illustrated Sydney News* of 1889.

In 1912 in the *Jubilee Souvenir of the Municipality of Newtown*, we read about *a large cottage surrounded with huge trees and a well-kept garden* [which was] *demolished some years ago*, the property now enclosed by Hordern's advertisement hoarding. It remembers the Judge and his daughter, *liberal and benevolent*, who *never turned a peddlar away*. On 11 December 1912, the *Sun*, an afternoon tabloid, featured an unsigned newspaper article about Eliza Donnithorne, which alongside other Sydney stories was later *collected, arranged and indexed* by William Henry George Freame in 1915 for his scrapbook of newspaper cuttings *Chronicles of the Past*. That article was a rehash of the earlier piece by a journalist identified only as a *Sun* man, who was supposed to have interviewed Thomas Clarke, the sexton of Newtown's St Stephen's church, who in turn claimed to have observed Miss Donnithorne since he was a child; Clarke – the child, like Pip, a voyeur of an adult world – once saw her wearing not a white dress, but *a big black shawl over her head.*

This must be the same William Freame who accompanied G.C.J. on his ramble in Newtown about 12 years earlier. And if I've researched correctly, he was the son of Ellen Jane Coker and William Henry Freame; his half-brother was the *illustrious adventurer, soldier, orchardist and interpreter* (and possibly spy) Wykeham Henry Koba Freame. I'd love to know more about these Freames, but not right now.

Regarding Eliza's failed wedding, the *Sun* man repeats: *How did our heroine bear the blow?* And answers: *Well it appears to have completely prostrated her, and it is to be feared, to some extent, affected her reason…she never again left the house. She appears to have lost all interest in life…her only solace being books. She became an insatiable reader, and when she died…she left an extensive and valuable library behind her.* In an article titled 'Dickens and Australia' (Parramatta and District Historical Society, 1923), Freame thought that Miss Havisham was *wrongly supposed by many to have been suggested by Miss Donnithorne.*

The story was repeated by G.A. King in a piece in the *Sydney Morning Herald* (18 June1927) about the restoration and maintenance of the grounds of Camperdown Cemetery. The *Brisbane Courier* (1 March 1928) ran a brief account titled *A Pathetic Love Story*, by a local historian Florence Eliza Lord, which tells how everything was ready for Eliza Donnithorne's marriage, *but the bridegroom arrived not*, and the *bride-elect* left her wedding preparations untouched and lived *in absolute retirement* until her death in 1886. I *have even heard that the poor carriage horses were kept confined to the stables until they grew almost too fat to walk.*

On *Sydney Morning Herald* and *Sydney Mail* letterhead in 1933 the same G.A. King, a journalist, historian and trustee of the Camperdown Cemetery, applied to the Registrar of Probates for a copy of Eliza's will for the purpose of an historical article. He claimed to have met a gentleman who in turn claimed to have witnessed Miss Donnithorne's signature to the document. He was informed a copy would cost £1 14 shillings.

The solicitor Henry Cox Colyer (1841–1889) who witnessed the will, was no longer alive at that time; he must have been a family friend, as Colyer's father John Godden Colyer had acquired land in Kiama at the same time as James Donnithorne had. H.C. Colyer's uncle (his mother's brother) was the eccentric artist Samuel Elyard (1817–1910), who died in Nowra. There's a watercolour by Elyard of *Mr Slades Milking Establishment, Newtown* (1877) with Camperdown Lodge very faintly on the horizon. Unfortunately the name of the other witness of her will is hard to read, it looks like I. James, but I haven't found him nor anything he might have said about his visit to Camperdown Lodge.

A loose scattering of facts is conglomerating. In the *Sydney Morning Herald* (5 January 1935), in an article titled 'Literary Link with Dickens', C.G.C. Christie (sometimes reprimanded for inaccuracies in other articles) wrongly states Judge Donnithorne was a great friend of Dickens.

Reminiscences of Newtown and Neighbourhood by George Henry Abbott (1867–1942) was published in 1937. As a child Abbott had lived opposite Camperdown Lodge, but offers little more than this: *Miss Donnithorne was still alive when I lived near her house, and I heard the story of how she was engaged to be married…the bridegroom did not appear* and *Miss Donnithorne never left the house until the time of her death.*

DID AN AUSTRALIAN STORY INSPIRE CHARLES DICKENS? asks a headline in the *Argus* (20 July 1940). Identifying (as if for the first time!) a *fascinating link* between *Great Expectations* and *a woman's grave in the cemetery at Camperdown*, it predicts one day *literary housemaids who spend their years carefully tidying the mysteries of other ages may touch* the controversy with *a literary feather duster and find the truth.*

Next, a staff correspondent of the *Sydney Morning Herald* (3 February 1948) reports that the Mitchell Library had acquired a Dickens manuscript – *seven small sheets of notepaper, bound in Morocco leather* – in which Dickens encouraged migration to Sydney. He points out that although the author was interested in Australia's *wild solitudes*, when invited to visit he declined the offer. The article mentions that the connection between Miss Havisham and Miss Donnithorne was unresolved.

A couple of weeks later, again in the *Sydney Morning Herald* (21 February 1948), historian and journalist Thomas Davies Mutch – a friend of the writer Henry Lawson, who is said to have *tried to wean Lawson from drink* – addressed the popular belief that Dickens had heard about Eliza from his sons who had been in Australia. He found that one son, Alfred Tennyson Dickens arrived in Australia in 1865, and his brother Edward Bulwer Lytton Dickens in 1869, and deduced that since *Great Expectations* was first serialised between 1860–61, its author could not have received the story from his sons. Mutch has his own theory: *as a result of some fascinating research I have discovered that Dickens did not know of Miss Donnithorne's existence, but based his famous character…on an experience which befell an innkeeper named Nathaniel Bentley*. When Bentley's bride died on the morning of her wedding in a fire, the bereft groom had the banquet room sealed up, never to be opened during his lifetime. And though he had once been a dandy, he stopped washing, lived in squalor and became known as Dirty Dick. Mutch concludes that it was not Eliza who inspired Dickens' story, but the reverse, it was the jilted bride in *Great Expectations* that created the legend of Eliza Donnithorne. His article is illustrated with a drawing of a Gothic entrance overgrown with branches and leaves, an open door, a dark interior, a boy delivering a letter, thrown back in shock by what he sees: which, we're left to assume, is that universal horror, a decaying bride.

When journalist George Blaikie writes his long and hammy article 'Mr Cuthbertson shoots through' in 1954, for a series called Our Strange Past, it is syndicated to a number of Australian publications. Adjectives abound. The girl is young and beautiful (of course), the night is *stilly*, Cuthbertson's horse trots *cautiously* towards the Newtown mansion. *Plumb terrified* her father would *aim a charge of light buckshot at his riding breeches*, he taps *nervously* at her shuttered window, calls her name *hoarsely*, she has a *feverish crack* at opening the shutter locks. *Mr Cuthbertson tensed in the saddle*. His wish: to see *the beauteous*

Eliza Emily…with heaving bosom and love light gleaming in her eye. Blaikie then has the couple wandering around at night and settling, *possibly on the nasturtiums*, with Cuthbertson keeping one eye open for Judge Donnithorne who *had a liver the size of a dinner plate and was in a perpetual state of near-explosion.* Father and daughter argue. Blaikie writes, I *will not rack your emotions with all the terrible scenes which took place.* The father gives in. Cuthbertson – *a very decent sort of young chap*, but confused – gets cold feet when the Judge swears *by the Bay of Bengal, if you fail my daughter in any way you shall pay for it.* Hearts stop and start. The wedding is planned and on the day, amidst flowers and sunshine, the bride *looked absolutely No. 1.* The feast? *Poultry, trifle, cream jelly, tarts…anything your hungry imagination cares to lay on the festive board.* Guests *in droves.* But evidently Cuthbertson had *shot through.* You know the rest, I'll cut Blaikie's long story short. He mentions *a romantically minded Sydney newspaper editor* who tried to get at the truth of it all in 1912, and tracked down Eliza's servants, only to be met with the phrase *our lips are sealed* (if this refers to the Bailey sisters and I'm not mistaken, one was dead, the other died that year). And he mentions the newspaper man's meeting with the very ancient sexton of St Stephen's (this sexton has a lot to answer for), who says it's *all bunkum…there wasn't any wedding arranged for any missing bridegroom…Because Miss Donnithorne became a recluse people decided there had to be a reason and provided a romantic one.* Blaikie concludes, *to this day, if you ask anyone in a Newtown pub about the judge's daughter you'll get the whole harrowing tale garnished with little modern touches such as 'they say she was the spittin' image of Jane Russell'.* And he gives his readers some parting advice, that if you hear these rumours you must appear to believe them, because Newtown has become a *mighty tough suburb*. Blaikie went on to write books titled *Wild Women of Sydney* (1980) and *Scandals Strange but True* (1984).

People love to repeat and embellish the story of Newtown's jilted bride. One version, by Elizabeth Birch on *charlesdickenspage.com*, tells of Eliza being laced into her corsets on the wedding day, with the clocks ticking and the sunlight fading; it has the Judge speaking to his daughter *gently* (contrasting Blaikie's image of the Judge roaring so loudly in anger that he could be heard in Melbourne); thereafter, people sometimes caught sight of the reclusive Eliza, dressed in black, on *a dark and moonless night*. But amidst all this speculation, Birch makes the point – a very good one – that Eliza *read widely... The mind that had avoided human contact for so long sought release in the printed page. She asked for nothing more of life than seclusion – to be left alone.*

In 1952 the antiquarian bookseller James Robert Tyrrell published his memoir *Old Books, Old Friends, Old Sydney*. Recounting his boyhood in Newtown, when Eliza Donnithorne's house was believed to be *haunted*, he stressed that this was *a strongly held Newtown belief*, and I *was still young enough to keep to the other side of the road in passing it, especially at night. Still, I would glance fearfully over to its front door, which, by night or day, was always partly open, though fastened with a chain.* He's not sure if at that time the house was inhabited or empty. On the other hand, a friend of his claimed that as a boy Tyrrell used to creep up to Eliza's house, open a shutter and *sometimes saw her moving about.* According to this account, it seems young Tyrrell watched closely enough to notice that only the dining room was in ruins, with the dusty wedding banquet set out on the table, but the rest of the house was well maintained. He even confirmed she was not wearing her wedding dress…*but the house was dark and she lived by candle light*, suggesting that her real eccentricity lay in turning night into day. Apparently Tyrrell had also met Eliza's servants, the Bailey sisters, who famously disclosed…nothing.

Odd commentary keeps turning up. On 5 May 1976 Robert H. Parr wrote for the Adventist *Record* that Eliza changed from being *as pretty as a picture* to becoming *a demented old recluse* because she had been waiting for the wrong Bridegroom.

In 1977 a textile artist crocheted a Miss *Donnathorne* [sic] with antique ribbons, sequins and beads.

In 1980 'The Legend (or Ballad) of Eliza Emily Donnithorne', lyrics and music by John Armstrong, was recorded for the Cobbers' album *Portraits of Australian Women*. It starts out like this – *She stands at the window watching the carriages/ Approaching the house in the spring of the year,/ She smiles at the people hurrying everywhere/ Lovely Eliza's wedding draws near* – and ends thirty years later, with the appearance of a horse-drawn hearse.

There's a *Sunday Telegraph* article in 1991, a full-page Historical Feature with a tacky illustration of a sour-looking Miss Donnithorne in wedding gear, encountering a snarling mouse near her cobwebbed wedding cake; the article is about Dickens' Australian connections. Full of fabrications and mistakes, it kicks off with Eliza *in 1854…considered one of the most eligible young ladies in Sydney.* For her wedding *a beautiful gown of lace, silk and satin was sewn by hand and a sumptuous breakfast feast was prepared.* It's a wonder that journalists never tired of rehashing these trashy details.

The entry for Eliza Emily Donnithorne in the *Australian Dictionary of Biography*, by academic J.S. Ryan, contains mistakes and will need to be updated. But it concludes sensibly that the identification of Eliza and Miss Havisham is *circumstantial.* Like Mutch, Ryan suggests that *Sydney people, after reading the novel, may have created the tradition by identifying Eliza with Miss Havisham.*

The conjoined and often rather camp Havisham-Donnithorne narrative has also opened up questions of sexuality and gender. In 2005 at *rootsweb.com*, Phil Giles conjectured that *Eliza Donnithorne was a man, a gay man. He arrived here in the mid-1800s with his father James Donnithorne aboard the Tiberius, the passenger list states that James*

Donnithorne, 43 years old, arrived with his son William, aged 12. The arrival records also show only two male Donnithornes and other stories have it that all his daughters died of cholera in Calcutta…It is little wonder the marriage never went ahead…If Dickens knew this then Great Expectations may have been more of a page turner than it turned out to be! When Giles is asked for verification, he gets cranky, replying: *Where is the evidence? It is in the passenger list for the Tiberius…(do you want me to say it for the third time?).* He adds that of course the judge did not like his *son canoodling* with his *friend* George Cuthbertson.

Giles' theory doesn't quite add up; with the assistance of staff at the Australian National Maritime Museum and the Mitchell Library, I found no ship called *Tiberius* in Australian waters around that time, and no such passenger list. But it's an interesting hypothesis, especially as Dickens played with ideas of gender in many of his novels. In *Great Expectations* he has Mrs Joe (herself a gender conundrum) asking: *'And she is a she, I suppose?… Unless you call Miss Havisham a he. And I doubt if even you'll go so far as that.'*

Eliza's story also lends itself to spook. In 2008 blogger Selma Tracey Sergent, who lived near Camperdown cemetery as a student, reflected on Eliza's fate. Selma, her neighbour Pearl, and the church caretaker were convinced that Eliza walked the cemetery grounds at night. *When Pearl's grandfather was a boy he had lived near Eliza's home…All the local children believed it was haunted and crossed the street rather than walk directly in front of it. Once Pearl's grandfather had peered through one of the windows and had seen a woman inside with long, bedraggled hair, moaning to herself...* [what a nuisance all those prowling, eavesdropping boys must have been for Eliza, it's a wonder she didn't scoop one up to roast like a witch in fairy tales]...*In 1920 Camperdown Lodge was burned to the ground and it was shortly after that local residents reported seeing a ghost in the cemetery.* Selma sees it too. *The shadows were dense. I felt if I stepped into the cemetery I would plunge into nothingness, into a place where I would instantly be lost.* And behold, Eliza appeared to the blogger who describes her: *her long, white dress dragging in the dirt.*

Others join in, contributing their own ghost sightings or gossip to Sergent's blog: that Eliza was pregnant and had a son who was adopted by the locally renowned Kelly family; that the groom was paid off or killed by her father, or that he eloped with a wealthier woman; that the smell from the rotting wedding banquet spread right down the street; that Eliza was a witch. One respondent kicks herself for not visiting *that cemetery when I was a student at Sydney Uni.* One says that even in her deepest grief she would not have let the banquet go to waste, *I'd have to get the glad wrap out and get that lot into the fridge.* Another agrees, but suggests tupperware.

The blog then features an entire article by Colbert Moore (*Sun*, early 1970s, no date), titled 'Jilted Bride Became Famous Newtown

Legend'. It's sent in by Alan. Here Eliza is *a raving beauty* with many suitors, including one called Cuthbertson. But *Judge Donnithorne who had a nasty liver, probably from too much curry and gin consumed in India, didn't like the idea of anyone taking his daughter from him*, which led to Eliza sneaking out of the house at night for *a kiss or two* and a lover in fear of his future father-in-law, who eventually gave in and the marriage was arranged for *a certain date in 1848.* There's a lot of innuendo (the curry, the kisses) and melodrama, such as making Eliza say: *No one shall touch the wedding feast. My bridegroom shall come back to me through that front door. Everything shall remain exactly as it is until he shall come!* And inane arguments between father and daughter about the door being left open for Cuthbertson's return. The father slams the door shut. She opens it again, leading to *the invasion of flies, mosquitoes, cats and dogs*. He warns her about thieves and murderers. So *she bought a huge and savage mastiff and tethered it in the hall as a guard dog*. The door remained open. After her father's death she secured the open door with a chain and became a recluse until her death. The contributor of Moore's article then recommends Godl's piece 'The Donnithorne's [sic] of Camperdown Lodge' – as *another great article…very thorough* – and provides the link.

If he existed, Colbert Moore was revisiting the article by the *Sun* man of 1912, who had himself relied on an earlier article in which a journalist claimed to have investigated the story, spoken to the sexton and found Eliza's servants, whose lips were then and still are *sealed to everyone and everything*, and told him…nothing. I've searched but I've not yet found Moore, apart from his appearance in Godl's novel *Eliza*. When I mention this to Godl in an email (and politely also point to the trail of errant apostrophes in all his texts, they were beginning to annoy me), he angrily terminates our correspondence. Clearly I'd overstepped the mark of email etiquette.

For a long time Godl's apparent authority – based on a collection of material, which he sometimes wrote up as short, chapter-like pieces – has dominated research into the life of Eliza Donnithorne. I don't know what motivated his pursuit of the Donnithornes, and I don't understand all the bees in his bonnet about some aspects of the story, such as illegitimacy, which he deals out in dollops of disgust, with expressions like *bastardy*, *a servant knocked up by her employer*, *born on the wrong side of the blanket*, etc. Now much of his collection is in Marrickville Public Library. It's there that I find the article in *The Sun*, undated, called 'Jilted Bride became famous Newtown Legend', and in handwriting just above the title, *by Colbert Moore*.

In his essay 'Eliza Emily Donnithorne's Great Expectations' (2003), Godl has the family descended from *untitled nobility whose ancestry extended back into the mists of time*…the father Nicholas *proudly* introducing his teenage son to the court of George III…and the son, James, *thunderstruck by the glamour and excess* of what he saw, making friends with the Prince Regent – *the two young dandy's* [sic] *became notorious in London for their misbehaviour.* Later James was compromised by *his scandal laden past and adulterous liaisons with Indian ladies, often resulting in pregnancies.* In Australia he turns into *an industrious man, an empire builder* and *the great joy of his life was always his daughter Eliza*…but when he tried to arrange marriages for her and she refused, it led to *intense friction between them, often going for days without speaking.* Godl then has Eliza attending bible study classes at St Stephen's in Newtown, along with other young women *forbidden careers due to their status* who were *killing time waiting for a suitable husband to come along.* In love with an unsuitable young man, Eliza *had to take to climbing out of her bedroom window.*

On a populist website about mysteries that includes stories about Steve Irwin, Harold Holt, Hubcap Larry, bushrangers and ghosts, there's an Eliza section by Paul Denham and Millie Ford, with additional information by John Sullivan and John Godl. Did it really take four people to describe for the umpteenth time, in rosy prose, the meeting between Eliza and Cuthbertson which was *the beginning of a romance written in heaven*? In which the class divide posed *an unbridgeable chasm* that led to *stolen moments in the wild pastures of Camperdown Cemetery* where *they were often spotted by the sexton.* And when her father went away on business *Eliza would send one of the trusted servants with a message to Mr Cuthbertson* who would then *ride out on horseback to Camperdown Lodge…like an American cowboy*. It's too much for me. I leave Godl to his own devices.

Oddly, looking for contemporaries who might have known Eliza or commented on her, I find that around that time one man did come riding in, kicking up the dust, but for a different girl. The English biologist and Darwinist, Thomas Henry Huxley, was in Sydney from late 1848 to early 1849 as assistant surgeon and naturalist on the *Rattlesnake*. He was putting all his flair into courting Henrietta Heathorn, a Newtown resident and his future wife. She was living with her sister's family at Holmwood, a white-columned Georgian house with beautiful grounds at the southern end of Cooks River Road; Holmwood Street is a reminder of where the house once stood. Henrietta was the one who'd commented that Stuart Alexander Donaldson did not lack self-esteem, so she might also have been acquainted with the Donnithornes. On his voyage back to England, it was Macauley's *History*, Lamartine's *Histoire des Girondins*, and especially Mrs Gaskell's *Mary Barton* that gave Huxley *many an hour's pleasure*. Did Huxley return to England with tales about Eliza, which in a roundabout way reached Dickens? Their circles must have overlapped; for one thing, both were interested in mesmerism, which Huxley saw as *retrospective prophecy*, a concept straddling science, history and fiction; Dickens, with his own penchant for the paranormal, for coincidences and the layering of realities, was a member of the Ghost Club (founded in 1862). Or was Charles

Darwin the missing link? Both Darwin and Dickens were members of the Athenaeum Club; and Darwin – mostly a reclusive person – found that reading Dickens cured his headaches. Was Eliza's story proffered in a gentleman's club, by prominent Englishmen such as these, with an interest in Australia?

In an article at *Sydney Archives' Newtown Project* website, called 'The Truth About The Truth About Eliza Donnithorne', Matt Murphy identifies Eliza as *one of the most famous people in Newtown's history* and tries to debunk a number of presumptions about her. For example, regarding the idea that Eliza was pregnant, and had been told the baby was stillborn, so that she was unaware it was being raised by a woman called Anne Kelly, Murphy points out that Kelly was James Donnithorne's maid, by whom he already had a son, and the child in question was their daughter Anna, born in 1845 (actually 1846).

Murphy observes that *even Dame Mary Gilmore waded into the story saying she visited Eliza Donnithorne in 1889...and that her father knew the intended groom well and that his career as an army officer was ruined by the ordeal.* Surprisingly, here we have an upset groom reintroduced into the puzzle. It means Eliza might well have been the jilter rather than the jilted.

While Murphy rejects Gilmore's tale, I'm wondering (since Eliza died May 1886) if Gilmore had mistaken the dates, but otherwise told the truth? Because we know that in early 1886, during her first visit to

Sydney, Gilmore (who was then still Mary Jean Cameron) stayed with her aunt, the teacher and feminist Jeannie Lockett in nearby Camperdown. Could Lockett have known Eliza and taken her niece to see her? In which case Eliza kept interesting company for a recluse. Maybe Gilmore just got her wires crossed, conflating two or more incidents.

One of James Donnithorne's Australian descendants kept newspaper cuttings of an exchange of letters to the editor, unfortunately without the date or name of the newspaper. The exchange begins with a letter from C. R. Ramage of Epping, who describes Eliza *Donnythorne's* stone house on the corner of King and Georgina Street where, he says, a grocery firm's premises now stands. Ramage then proceeds to tell the usual story from jilting via the eternally mouldering wedding breakfast to seclusion, mentions Dickens, and Miss Havisham, and the cemetery.

In reply, Mary Gilmore of King's Cross writes, rather imperiously, as was her manner, I *am perhaps the only person left alive who saw and remembers Miss Donnithorne*. She recounts her time spent in Newtown in 1888–89, when she was working at a girls' school in Stanmore and boarded at Cambridge Terrace, and was *attracted to the beautifully built cottage where Miss Donnithorne lived… I called to ask for a street I wanted to find. Miss Donnithorne answered the door (on a chain)*. Ever forthright, Gilmore called again two months later. *This time she opened the door, and I saw a still red-headed woman, with strongly marked features and a bad temper.* Gilmore was told to get out and never come back! When I tell this to the historian Chrys Meader, she says Eliza was waited on by servants all her life, and would not have answered her own door.

Once more Gilmore says she saw Eliza, from afar, *getting into a hansom*. She and a younger woman *were beautifully richly dressed for a party or dinner*. She was told *by old residents of Newtown* that the women *went out a lot at night, even to Government House, but not in the daytime.* Gilmore goes on to claim her family had known and liked *the defaulting bridegroom... a captain in the Army...* [whose] *career was ruined*. With a pinch of scepticism, Gilmore, however, does not believe the story of the wedding feast left on the table, she reckons Sydney's ants and flies would have eaten it all.

A squashed Mr Rammage apologised for his incorrect spelling of the name Donnithorne. There's another letter, from Mrs Fernance of Blacktown. Her mother was Miss Donnithorne's niece, who had visited her aunt many times, and had passed on the following information to her family: that Eliza was very wealthy and lived a quiet and retired life, no food was left to rot but the table setting was kept for many years, she dressed normally, and there was speculation that as *the groom was in the habit of carrying large sums of money, he might have been waylaid.*

I double-check some of Gilmore's claims with a couple of elders of Australian literature, and the response is unanimous: she made things up all the time. One says, *She was a bit of a fantasist. She claimed to know all sorts of people she could not have met, and to be present at events that took place before her birth…She also claimed that various people (eg Henry Lawson) were in love with her…Most people who knew her tended to pass over this aspect of her personality rather kindly as a bit of grande dame grandstanding.* He concluded, I *should think the Eliza Donnithorne story…would come into this category.*

But to return to Matt Murphy's article, he had been in touch with one Australian great-granddaughter of Eliza's niece, descended from Ann Kelly Jones and James Donnithorne, who thought her relative was not eccentric, that in those days it was usual to leave doors open and chained, moreover it was fashionable for women to wear white dresses that resembled wedding attire, and common practice to have tables always set for the next meal. After searching St Stephen's church records from 1845–1865 for the Donnithorne marriage banns, and drawing a blank, Murphy concludes *there was no groom, there was no wedding. There was just an old spinster, possibly eccentric, possibly living with her faithful servants. If sources can be believed, she was an avid reader as the only people she met at the front door, with the exception of the local clergy, were those selling books.*

A Squalor Survivors website features Eliza in a list of famous squalorees alongside the unkempt and sloppy Beethoven and the seriously non-domestic Edith and Edie Bouvier Beale. It's another version of Eliza Emily Donnithorne, this time as the Queen of Grunge.

An opera called *Miss Donnithorne's Maggot* by Peter Maxwell Davies, with a libretto by Randolph Stow, is regarded by those who have heard it as either truly magnificent or excruciatingly awful. That's *maggot* as in *whim*, though obviously the word also retains its grubbier connotations. The opera was commissioned by the Adelaide Festival of Arts and first performed in 1974; it's dedicated to Patrick White. One Stow specialist tells me that White took it as a compliment and was *quite surprised but pleased...also because Miss Donnithorne was such a typical 'White-type' spinster figure.* Stow himself was a solitary person; he lived for many years in Suffolk, a place later epitomised by W.G. Sebald for its lonely landscapes. In his introductory note, Stow admits that the work *is a slur on the reputation of an unfortunate lady. How she behaved in the extraordinary privacy of her own home can never be known to us. But neighbours will talk; and Miss Donnithorne, by her way of life, positively threw down the gauntlet to hers...How Dickens heard of her we do not know*, but – Stow explains – she outlived him and being a great reader, *she was probably well acquainted with her fictional counterpart.*

A note for the production in 1994 of *Miss Donnithorne's Maggot* by the New Chamber Opera, suggests that Stow's interpretation is *akin to the psychological case studies...strongly favoured by the Viennese 'Expressionists'...The text represents the morbid, often violent fantasies of a recluse, with particular focus on the denial of her desire for sexual defloration.* She rants, raves, reels, she fantasises rape, and Davies directs her to *noisily tear off pieces of cake (which are made of cardboard) from time to time*. A review of a performance in March 2003 by the Zeitgenössische Oper in Berlin notes *siren-like shooting violin glissandi* and *ticking and rustling xylophone chatter*, with *a hint of Monty Python in the air*. There's also an opera called *Miss Havisham's Fire* (1979) by Dominick Argento, libretto by John Olon-Scrymgeour. A musical-theatre version of Eliza's life, titled *Die alternde Braut* (The Aging Bride) was performed in 2009 in Mönchengladbach in Germany.

When Simon Caterson reviewed Angus Calder's *Gods, Mongrels and Demons*, an essayistic parade of eccentrics, he suggested that rather than expressing extremes of vengeance, *Eliza most likely did nothing at all for the best part of three decades*. Caterson thought Samuel Beckett would have been the best interpreter of her inertia. ('The Real Miss Havisham?', *Sunday Age*, 7 March 2004).

In 2007 radio announcer John Laws published *There's always more to the story: John Laws' favourite Australian stories*, which mentions *the adventures of the eccentric Miss Donnithorne*. More recently, Graham Seal, professor of folklore at Curtin University, included the *larger than life character…sad Eliza Donnithorne* in his *Great Australian Stories* (2010), alongside numbskulls, yowies, bunyips, and Dad and Dave. Another addition to the craze, in 2011, is *Lost Expectations – The Real Miss Haversham* [sic] by Alan Wardrope. Eliza now has the status of folk heroine. A play called *Princess*, with a script by Melody Parker, was performed recently at the Camden Fringe Festival (UK), again loosely based on the Eliza story, with a heroine named Lily Fortune.

The Donnithorne family papers at the State Library of NSW contain personal correspondence and other papers concerning sheep, cattle, business, as well as a stack of letters to Eliza from her English financial advisors. There is also, without explanation, a Report of the Select Committee on the Proposed Overland Route to Port Essington, dated 1843. Ludwig Leichhardt led his first expedition to Port Essington in 1844–45. He was thought to have perished on this expedition, and upon his incredible return became an instant hero. On 15 July 1846 he attended Sir George Gipps' departure from the colony. Perhaps someone pointed him out to Eliza, who had only arrived in Sydney three weeks earlier.

I need not recall to the recollection of those here present, the surprise, the enthusiasm, and the delight, with which your sudden appearance in Sydney was hailed, about six months ago. The surprise was about equal to what might be felt at seeing one who had risen from the tomb, said the Honourable Speaker of the Legislative Council in September 1846, at a ceremony to reward Leichhardt and his fellow expeditioners with £1000 *in consideration of the successful issue of that very perilous enterprise* and for services rendered in the interests of science and the colony, for they had opened up land that could now *become the abode of civilised man* (this notion of *civilised man* is rolled out more than once) and had cut a path to the Indian Ocean, *which would appear to render the Australian continent a mere extention of the Anglo-Indian empire.* Newspapers reported the speech and Leichhardt's reply (he was *evidently deeply affected*) in full. I imagine that Eliza either read about this ceremony, or that she attended it with her father, because the establishment of ports in Australia's far north, to facilitate trade with India, China and the rest of the world was a subject close to James Donnithorne's heart. It was believed that Port Essington would become *a great commercial entrepot.*

The German explorer then used his new status to socialise with the city's wealthiest merchants and their families, to raise more money for his next expedition. It's possible that James Donnithorne was one of his subscribers. With the intention of crossing the country east to west, he set out on another expedition in 1848 and never returned. Just down the road from Camperdown Lodge was Leichhardt Lodge, owned by William Aldis, the tobacconist and friend of Leichhardt who had first recognised the explorer in the street after his miraculous return in 1845, and mourning his loss after 1848, had named his house after him. In a relaxed moment, recently, while I was rereading Patrick White's *Voss*, a novel based largely on the life of Leichhardt, White's heroine Laura Trevelyan took on an Eliza-like identity. White describes her as *someone for whom the keenest torment or exhilaration was, in fact, the most private*, that she *read a great deal* and that the young men did not care for her, because she was *given to reading books*; I even thought the

Cornish surname, Trevelyan, was a clue. But no, I'm not suggesting that Eliza was in love with Ludwig and waiting for his return, or that White knew something we don't know. It was just a whim.

Eavesdroppers 2: What Really Happened

Something stirred in an adjoining chamber; it would not do to be surprised eavesdropping; I tapped hastily and as hastily entered.
Charlotte Brontë, *The Professor*

Charlotte Brontë wrote her first novel, *The Professor*, in 1846 (published 1857) after she had returned from Brussels, *sick with a private unhappiness for which there was no cure* (to quote the critic Margaret Lane). She was suffering from heart-sickness. It was both a private pain and an epidemic taking hold of men and women in *adjoining chambers* – hearts, houses, novels – across the nineteenth century and around the globe. Locked in their various solitudes, people eavesdropped on each other's heartache, and on other personal mysteries, by reading books. Reading and overhearing are much alike, both pursued quietly, both a form of epistemophilia, a love of knowledge. It felt like I was eavesdropping on Eliza when I went to the Mitchell Library to look at the letters sent to her in Sydney between 1846 and 1881, from her financial advisors John Chalmers and James Boulton Pratt in London, mostly about shares, remittances and dividends, which didn't interest me much; I was looking for more personal information.

Chalmers often alludes to the possibility that Eliza and her father will return to England and regrets they are still in Australia. From as early as 1851 there's constant mention of her health, it seems she was often unwell. Then we hear of the *melancholy event of the death of your father*, acknowledging that she suffered great stress while taking care of her *departed parent*.

Both Chalmers and Pratt express constant concern for Eliza's health. But I can discern nothing more specific than severe and chronic headaches. In the absence of medical records, we can only guess what was ailing her. Influenced by rumours that she never went outside during the day, I've wondered, for example, if she suffered from some kind of photosensitivity; perhaps a form of porphyria.

But despite her illness, another picture emerges unexpectedly from the correspondence, of a woman very much in control of her own financial situation, who also keeps in touch with and sends presents and money to family and friends, and is compassionate and charitable towards those asking for help. For days I'm in the library on microfilm until closing time. It's not always easy to decipher the handwriting, some parts of some letters I pore over for hours, and the findings are often mundane. When I learn that occasionally Eliza sent newspaper cuttings to her correspondents, and greeting cards to Pratt's children, I'm stopped by the absolute ordinariness of these facts, and walk to Wynyard station in the dark, in heavy winter rain.

A week later my husband and I emerge from the ruin of Pope's Grotto in Twickenham in high summer sunshine. I'd brought my composite image of Eliza with me, in note form, with the idea of gathering more material. But travel disperses the imagination in strange ways.

We eat flat *Saturn* peaches, as we walk along the sandy gravel towpath that follows the bank of the Thames. A new culinary fad, these peaches are everywhere; a newspaper article suggests it's a peach that preserves your dignity. And as the day was fine, and we had an hour or two on our hands, we crossed the river by the ferry – from the Middlesex to the Surrey side – and stroll along the footpath through some meadows, eventually heading towards tea at Ham House (apologies to Dickens, *Little Dorrit*, chapter 17).

In the early 1720s the writer and traveller Lady Mary Wortley Montagu, living at nearby Saville House, strolled those paths. She told her sister, I *see sometimes Mr Congreve, and very seldom Mr Pope who continues to embellish his house at Twickenham. He has made a subterranean grotto, which he has furnished with looking glasses.* The grotto was once a trove of mirrors and lamplight, shells, marbles, stalactites, crystals, Cornish diamonds. A geological encyclopaedia stuck to the walls of a basement and underground passages. A dream. Pope describes how *I have found a spring of the clearest water, which falls in a perpetual Rill, that echoes thru' the Cavern day and night… When you shut the Doors of this Grotto, it becomes on the instant, from a luminous Room, a Camera Obscura, on the walls of which all the objects of the River, Hills, Woods, and Boats, are forming a moving Picture.* After her quarrel with Pope, Lady Mary thought his cave was a foggy, damp and smelly place. Dr Johnson also made fun of Pope's *excavation*. It must have been on one of those sandy paths that a young Horace Walpole overtook Alexander Pope one day, and the Neoclassical idea gave way to the Gothic.

Alfred Lord Tennyson lived in Twickenham from 1851 to 1853. He complained of too many visitors. On 11 August 1852, Tennyson wrote to his friend Elizabeth Barrett Browning *to tell you what I am sure your woman's and poet's heart will rejoice in, that my wife was delivered of a fine boy at 9.30 a.m. this day…I never saw any face so radiant with all high and sweet expression as hers when I saw her some time after*. Barrett Browning – who had been reclusive for much of her adult life, due to illness – remembered the birth of her own son, now three years old, and replied *with the memory of all that ecstasy as I felt it myself, still thrilling through me*. In 1903, Tennyson's son Hallam became Australia's second Governor-General.

In the 1850s the Russian writer Alexander Herzen spent some of his exile years in Twickenham and Richmond.

From 1855 to 1859 Mary Ann Evans (the writer George Eliot) and

George Lewes lived in Richmond, where Eliot worked on her first novel *Scenes of Clerical Life* and began her second, *Adam Bede*. Central to this book is the caddish figure of Captain Arthur Donnithorne. Curiously, it seems that Eliot had taken her *nom de plume* from George Donnithorne Elliott, a lieutenant with the 33rd Regiment of the Bengal Native Infantry, who drowned in Lake Nainital in July 1854 (some records suggest other dates of death). Had she read about it in the paper, or had she known him or his family? As a journalist in the *New-York Tribune* noted on 24 February 1906, *it seems very hard to believe that there was no connection between the pseudonym of George Eliot and the personality of Mr George Donnithorne Elliott who died just three years before 'Adam Bede' was published.* Eliot herself claimed *Adam Bede* was based on a story of real events, told by her aunt. Another journalist in the *Auckland Star* on 6 September 1902 wondered what the author was concealing under her pseudonym, tells the story of the drowned officer, and that *he probably left Warwickshire for India when George Eliot was some seventeen years of age* and *more than once returned to England*, but leaves the rest to our imagination. George Eliot was born in Nuneaton, Warwickshire. Major General Patrick Maxwell, in *Pribbles and Prabbles* (1906) goes one step further: *who knows but that George Donnithorne Eliot [sic]...was an early friend, flame, or ideal of Marian Evans*, hence her adoption of his name. Did she also, I wonder, enshrine the end of that relationship in the drowning of her hero and heroine of her novel

The Mill on the Floss (1860): *The next instant the boat was no longer seen upon the water, and the huge mass was hurrying on in hideous triumph…the boat reappeared, but brother and sister had gone down in an embrace never to be parted, living through again in one supreme moment the days when they had clasped their little hands in love and roamed the daisied fields together.*

I haven't disentangled the connection between the drowned man and his middle name Donnithorne: his father was Charles Elliott (1777), his mother Alicia Boileau (1779), who were married in Calcutta in 1802. There were Elliotts and Boileaus in Bengal who would have crossed paths with the Donnithornes; it appears that Charles Elliott was judge and magistrate in Fatehgarh c1810–13 (his house was struck by lightning and destroyed in 1812); the families may have been close enough for the boy, George Elliott, born 1815, to be given Donnithorne as a middle name.

In Richmond and Twickenham, Lewes and Eliot – whom he called Polly – liked to go for walks; perhaps they talked of pseudonyms and characters and prototypes. They must also have talked of shares: in 1860, to supplement the income she earned from writing, Lewes purchased *95 shares in the Great Indian Peninsular Railway for Polly*. The couple later bought other domestic and colonial stocks, in Canada, India, Australia and South Africa.

Half a century later, Leonard and Virginia Woolf were also

walkers on these paths. Their move to Hogarth House, Paradise Road, Richmond in early 1915 coincided with the publication of Woolf's first novel, *The Voyage Out*. Leonard Woolf was a great supporter of Indian independence. Through her father's first wife, Virginia was related to the Thackeray family, and her mother Julia Prinsep Stephen, née Jackson, was born in India, as was her great-aunt, the photographer Julia Margaret Cameron; the family, especially on the Prinsep side, was steeped in British East India Company history. Woolf's great-uncle Henry Thoby Prinsep was Secretary to the Government of India; he was the official to whom James Donnithorne was answerable as salt agent, who decided on James' pay cut and signed off on his resignation. In her novel *Night and Day* (1919), the heroine – burdened by her family's past, trying to break free – recalls how *There were always visitors – uncles and aunts and cousins 'from India', to be reverenced for their relationship alone, and others of the solitary and formidable class, whom she was enjoined by her parents to 'remember all your life'*. Her greatest work, *The Waves* (1931) builds this drama of defining the self – of solitudes and communalities, imperialisms, nationalisms, militarisms – to a crescendo. If Eliza had been a character, Virginia Woolf would have been her best author.

With some of the guineas left from the sale of the tenth pearl of her string, the heroine of Woolf's novel *Orlando* (1928) buys herself *a complete outfit of such clothes as women then wore* and after a long absence sails for England. Unlike Orlando, and despite the urging of friends and family to come home, Eliza decided to stay in Sydney.

After her father's death, Eliza retained a number of servants. Most important – though it's uncertain when they came to work for her – were Sarah Ann Bailey who in 1852 was aged twenty-two, and her sister Ellen Elizabeth aged twenty; they were born at Montpeliers Farm in Writtle near Chelmsford, Essex. I wonder if Eliza met them when they made a hat for her, because in the Sands Directory I find *Bailey, Misses*, listed as Milliners, living on Newtown Road in 1858. If Eliza spoke only to a triumvirate of clergyman, solicitor and physician, and to occasional booksellers, then the clergyman was probably Rev. Kemp, her father's executor, who died in 1874, and in later years his successor Rev. Robert Taylor, who was curate at St Stephen's in 1866, then officiating minister in 1868, and incumbent in 1870. Possibly they involved her in plans and finances for a new church in the grounds of Camperdown cemetery.

Her doctor was James Cox. I'm assuming this was James Charles Cox (1834–1912), born at Mulgoa, where in 1841–42 the family built Fernhill – a beautiful sandstone house in a style sometimes called Old Colonial Grecian, designed by Mortimer Lewis, whose work included the court houses at Darlinghurst, Hartley, Berrima and Parramatta. Cox was educated at the King's School in Parramatta, studied medicine in Edinburgh and returned home to register as a medical practitioner in NSW in 1859. He was one of the leading doctors in Sydney, a Fellow of the Royal College of Surgeons, and of the Royal Society. His address was 73 Hunter Street, Sydney. From 1883–1912 he taught medicine at the University of Sydney. A natural historian with a strong interest in conchology, he was a trustee of the Australian Museum and in 1881–82 president of the Linnaean Society of NSW. He owned many Australian and Pacific Island artefacts, which he exhibited at Sydney's International Exhibition in 1879, and later sold. A close friend of William John Macleay, he presented some important Aboriginal bark paintings from the Port Essington region to the Macleay Museum.

We know from her will that Eliza had a *collection of curiosities*, though we don't know its content or size. She might have set aside a room, or a cabinet, or individual boxes. These kinds of collections are museum-like, theatre-like, ark-like miniature worlds, *aides memoires*, archives of knowledge, or of conjecture and fantasy. Had she always been acquisitive, and inquisitive? Already as a child in India and England – a keeper of small, portable oddities, feathers in hatbands, ferneries in bell-jars, beetles in matchboxes, marbles, bibelots, perhaps an item she'd purchased at Strawberry Hill's Great Sale in 1842? I check the *Aedes Strawberrianae* which lists the buyers, but there's no Donnithorne; a Mr Thorne bought a miniature of Lady Wortley Montagu as a Shepherdess, among other delights. Henry Bevan, of Cambridge House (possibly related to the Rev. Thomas Bevan), bought an Antique Marble Sarcophagus, for his garden.

Or did she start collecting in Australia? Far from the parsimonious habits often associated with reclusion, Eliza's collection points to the pleasures of discovery, identification and classification of individual items, and the augmentation, encyclopaedism and potential infinitude of the collection as a whole. She must have liked certain kinds of objects and had a sense of their beauty and variety. In *The Poetics of Space*, in a discussion of filing cabinets and drawers as spatial metaphors, Bachelard identifies our urge to collect, to put away, and to remember, consequently to control and be controlled by the order we choose to create, as key aspects of *the philosophy of having*. The cultural theorist Jean Baudrillard has characterised collecting as a *process of passionate abstraction* [which] *we call possesssion*. So when Dickens calls his heroine Miss Havisham and her house Satis House, he is stressing *Great Expectations* as a psychological and social narrative of *having*, with Miss Havisham tragicomically as the principal item of her own collection.

It's in this spirit that I have gathered and investigated and imagined Eliza's history…biography as vastness, minuteness, contiguity, and as a form of *Wunderkammer*.

Perhaps Eliza shared her interests and exchanged items – shells, nests, rocks, insects, artefacts – with James Cox. Clearly he was both her doctor and her friend. In one letter her English correspondent observes, *from what you write of your Doctor I think he understands your case*. There are no further clues to what her *case* might be.

We know Eliza bought books from William Maddock at 383 George Street; perhaps he and other sellers sent her their catalogues, or called on her at Camperdown Lodge with their latest selections. A leading bookseller and publisher – in 1868 he published Cox's *A Monograph of Australian Land Shells* – Maddock was also responsible for setting up circulating libraries. Through Maddock, Eliza may also have known, or known of, the poet Henry Kendall, and the Cornish newspaper publisher Samuel Bennett, who lived in Newtown in the 1860s.

While she settled her father's business affairs, Eliza's health did not improve. Chalmers managed her investments in England and with almost every letter urged her to *come home*. Beyond her front gate, Australian society was undergoing rapid changes. The Sydney-Parramatta Railway opened in 1855, and Newtown soon had a service of ten steam trains per day. That year, regarding the discovery of gold and the recent riot in the goldfield town of Ballarat, Karl Marx thought *the latest news from Australia adds a new element to the general discomfort, unrest and insecurity*. He likened the events of the Eureka Stockade to the American Declaration of Independence, and expected a revolution. Close to Camperdown Lodge, the first new building of the University of Sydney, designed by Edmund Blacket, was completed in 1857 and some of its teachers lived in Newtown, where the main street soon had *an important appearance similar to that of many villages in the neighbourhood of London. There are good shops, chapels, roadside residences…a postoffice, railway station and the terminus of a whole line of omnibuses.*

Chalmers was *sorry indeed that your health continues so delicate…you appear much depressed in spirits which is detrimental to your getting well* and observed that she possesses wealth – recently increased by £10,000 left by her late *excellent brother* William – but not health, and regrets that she is *only toiling for others to enjoy it.* He urges her not to waste her best years in a foreign land. When Eliza attempts to claim a property that once belonged to her grandfather, she encounters her brother Edward's opposition and his threats of legal challenge; the advisor asks why she would bother since she was wealthy enough. She suffers badly from headaches.

After the Donnithornes left Fatehgarh in the early 1820s, except for famine in 1837, some illegal practices of suttee, and the metalling of the main road, for the next few decades life in the garrison town, according to its chronicler Wallace, was *monotonously calm*. He mentions a few local eccentrics, like the Hon. F. J. Shore, who sported a long beard, dressed in local costume, displayed stuffed animals around his house, and kept two tame bears who dined with him. There were some scandals, one caused by an English girl who eloped with Nawab Sarbaland Khan, and a minor miracle in 1840, when a statue of Shiv appeared in Pargana Araritpur; the following year lightning caused a great fire in Farrukhabad, and in 1843 it rained chunks of meat.

Wallace says *nothing occurred at Fatehgarh to interfere with the daily routine down to the Mutiny of 1857.*

Eliza would have read in the *Sydney Morning Herald* about *events that have recently convulsed the Indian Empire* and *atrocities that have seldom been surpassed.* At the end of May in 1857, in an atmosphere thick with rebellion, Indian troops from Fatehgarh killed three British officers, followed by uprisings in other towns, which led to atrocities and counter-atrocities, including the Siege of Cawnpore (now Kanpur), where 120 captured women and children were hacked to death, dismembered and thrown into a well. This violence against British women and children – the *Angels of Albion* – was perceived as striking at the domestic heart of British imperialism and was reported emotively, with eyewitness accounts of a massacre scene that left behind blood-spattered hair, dresses, and bonnets. These horrific events are now variously referred to as the First War of Independence, or the Indian or Sepoy Mutiny; they marked the end of Company rule in India, and the beginning of the British Raj.

Eliza's eighteen-year-old niece Mary Penelope Donnithorne, who was six when her aunt left England, had married Edward Archer Wilde at Trinity Church in Twickenham in August 1858; he was called to the bar in November. A few years later, on Wednesday 26 March 1862 at Sunbury, she started to write recipes in a notebook with a blue marbled cardboard cover.

Looking for information about Mary Penelope, I found the book of recipes listed for auction on the internet. I contacted the auction house, the book had sold, but I pleaded my case – just to know what it looked like and contained – which was passed on to the person who bought it, who in turn passed my request to a friend, to whom it had been given as a gift; she collects old, handwritten cookbooks and likes to try old recipes. To my astonishment and great pleasure, this collector-and-cook sent me the book. On light blue pages in neat black ink, it has an Index to Recipes, paginated and listed 1 to 66. Mary Penelope Wilde started her book with the sunny optimism of Orange Jam. *Peel the oranges very thin; boil the peels in salt and water, till very tender, and afterwards in plain water: beat them in a mortar to a pulp: Take all the pips and pith from the oranges, and then mash them well: to every pound of fruit and peel, one pound of sugar. Boil till it is perfectly clear, and will set well.* I have tried to translate this as good instruction for the writing of my book. I see the last entries, numbers 34 to 36, are dedicated to treatments for Weak Eyes, Bedsores, and Toothache; they're dated 1889, the year Edward Archer Wilde died.

With much pomp Sydney University's Great Hall was opened on 18 July 1859. If Eliza had been sociable she could have gone to watch the gargoyles being carved. Her brother appears to have continued to challenge her over inheritance and in 1860 Eliza was informed that *the will case has at last been heard* and the result was not in her favour.

The Literary Intelligence section of the *Sydney Morning Herald* on 8 October 1861 noted that *Mr Dickens' story of 'Great Expectations,' now appearing in the pages of* All the Year Round, *is to be concluded in the number for the 3rd of August, and the following week Sir Edward Bulwer-Lytton will commence a new tale, entitled 'A Strange Story,' to be completed in six months.* It's likely that Eliza read the paper, even that she subscribed to *All the Year Round*, and had relished the serialisation which featured her supposed *Doppelgänger*. Was Dickens her favourite author? Or did she rather find her touchstones in the novels of the Brontës, and read about their reclusion in Elizabeth Gaskell's *Life of Charlotte Brontë*? Was she reading George Eliot's *Adam Bede*, surprised to find the seducer was a Captain Arthur Donnithorne? Or was she more interested in science than in literature?

When Prince Albert died in 1861, Queen Victoria wrote to Lord Palmerston: *The Queen feels her life ended, in a worldly point of view.* In deep mourning and relative seclusion, she lived as a widow for another forty years, in her own words *the most utterly wretched and desolate life that can be imagined.* She too was a reader; Mrs Oliphant, Jane Austen and Sir Walter Scott are said to have been among her favourite authors.

On 12 December 1862 Newtown became a municipality. It was *a favourite place of residence for gentlemen having businesses in Sydney.* The only drawback was the main road, which was not surfaced and either very dusty, or covered in mud. More buildings had been added to the University of Sydney. Caroline Chisholm opened a school for girls at Rathbone House on Stanmore Road. The area's first public school opened in 1863.

I read the letters from Chalmers and Pratt to Eliza on microfilm, and made notes of what was interesting and easily legible. A more careful reading – with the help of a magnifying glass and slow guesswork – gave me a few more pieces for the puzzle and threw up more questions. I must have been tired the first time I'd looked at the letter from Chalmers dated 26 February 1863. Now my eyes popped out when I read: *My solicitor says (and I hold with him) that as no Marriage was contemplated at the time the Release was drawn it was unnecessary to introduce it, but I wish from my heart such was the case and to one worthy of your warm heart*... He then goes on as usual, to discuss other *money matters*. Aged 41 in early 1863, had Eliza, who was often unwell, been recently engaged? It's possible, of course, but there are no other leads. More likely, this passage refers to a *Marriage not contemplated* some time in the past, perhaps as far back as the mismatch with Donaldson in 1848. It's hard to decipher the passage, perhaps she had asked Chalmers about the legal need for a *Release* (from some kind of verbal promise?) in relation to property she owned when marriage was (briefly?) on the agenda, perhaps her father had made a commitment to a groom of his choice (the *8,000 reasons* the Member for Durham required to marry her). It could also be the case, since she had referred this matter to her advisor and his solicitor in England, that romance was in the air, with someone unworthy, before she came to Australia, and she jilting him, or he jilting her, this was over and done with when she arrived in Sydney in 1846.

Chalmers' subsequent letters regret Eliza is so far away from her *anxious aunt and cousin* who would be happy to look after her. From his letters it appears her health is extremely unstable; in 1863 her illness is described as *severe*. There's mention of plans for extensive house repairs, but since she did not own Camperdown Lodge, this could be a reference to another Sydney property, maybe one she wanted to sell, which needed to be fixed up first. The tension with her brother over inheritance continues. In December 1863, Chalmers asked *when you are restored to health I would like very much to have a Photograph of your good self if it can be got without going from home to procure it.*

It appears that in 1864 she intended to travel to England with her doctor and his wife, but this idea fell through. Chalmers is *sorry to find you were suffering so much discomfort owing to your painful complaint* and suggests her nephew Edward should bring her home to get the best medical advice and *return you to the good health you enjoyed when you left us, for <u>well</u> did you look at that period*; the underlining is his. Chalmers health had been deteriorating and James Boulton Pratt takes over as her financial advisor.

Eliza's niece Henrietta Maria Donnithorne married Henry

Carnsew, a solicitor, at Twickenham's Holy Trinity Church in March 1864. They lived in his extensive mansion – *in the Domestic Gothic style* – at Somers in Sussex; their daughter Rosamund Isabella Charlotte was born in February 1865; Henrietta died later that year. At his own expense, Carnsew had been restoring the very old church of St Mary's in nearby Billingshurst and establishing a school there; when he ran into financial difficulties, he went to Brussels, where he seems to have worked as a journalist or translator. Rosamund went to live with her grandfather Edward Harris Donnithorne and his second wife Georgina at Colne Lodge.

The Wildes – Edward Archer and Mary Penelope – were living there too, or nearby, because in August 1865 their infant son died at Colne Lodge. How did Mary Penelope find solace for the deaths of her son and sister? In her book of recipes, on *Sept 30th '65*, she bravely writes out what's required to make a Wellington Pudding.

If Eliza read the paper on Thursday 25 May 1865, the report of a cyclone killing 60,000 and devastating Calcutta and nearby towns and villages, with a thirty-foot tidal wave racing up the Hugli river, would have recalled her childhood in Contai. The event, which had happened on 5 October 1864, was likened to the destruction of Pompeii or the Lisbon earthquake, one of history's great calamities. In his story 'City of Dreadful Night' (1888), Rudyard Kipling wrote, *Men have played with the Hughli as children play with gutter-runnel, and, in return, the Hughli once rose and played with men and ships till the Strand Road was littered with the raffle and carcasses of big ships.*

The City of Sydney Assessment Books for 1867, for Fitzroy Ward (now Potts Point), show that Eliza owned 114 Victoria Street, a three-storey, eight-room, brick and shingle house; it brought £80 per year in rent; Sir Stuart A. Donaldson also owned a house in Victoria Street.

In Chalmers' letters to Eliza there were constant references to Maria Dawes' concern for Eliza. Her husband Henry Dawes had been a Collector in Etawah and he was one of the executors of Captain Bampton's will; they lived in London at Hyde Park Gardens; Henry died in 1869, Maria in 1870.

The 1871 census shows that Rosamund Isabella Carnsew, aged about six, was living at Colne Lodge with her grandfather Edward and his wife; Edward's son Arthur Bampton also lived there, as well as five servants and a nurse, Agnes Crundell. In May of that year Rosamund's father Henry Carnsew, who had recently remarried, submits a petition *praying that his daughter, who is six years of age and a ward of Court, might be delivered over to his care and guidance as her natural guardian, by Mr Donnithorne, her maternal grandfather, with whom she had for some time past resided.* The judge said it was a *painful case*, but pointed out that it was against the law to take a ward abroad, and since Rosamund was being well maintained and educated by her grandfather, she should continue to stay with him. By 1881 Henry Carnsew was living in Hursley,

Hampshire, with his second wife Hilda Maria Agnes née Worsley and their ten-year-old daughter, also Hilda, who was born in Belgium.

In 1871–72 the novelist Anthony Trollope visited NSW and Sydney and famously declared that the city's beauty was beyond words. I *have seen nothing equal to it…nothing second to it…Sydney is one of those places…one cannot leave without a pang and tear – such is its loveliness.*

Gas lamps were erected along the Newtown Road and brickyards established at the southern end. An organ builder, a carpenter, and a wood turner had moved into Eliza's immediate neighbourhood. The new St Stephen's church, completed in 1871, was yet another significant Gothic Revival building designed by Edmund Blacket; it's said he *bestrode the Sydney architectural scene like a colossus.* Eliza's servants might have gone to watch the balloon ascent in nearby Victoria Park in January 1871, and described it for her.

When the property she'd inherited, Montmorency north-east of Melbourne, was threatened by local developments, and authorities tried to force a partial sale for lower than the market value, it was reported in the *Argus* on 5 August 1875 that Miss Donnithorne *refused to come to any compromise with respect to the compensation for the land required for a new road to Greensborough.* Her health fluctuated between *improving* and *alarming.* She sent a wedding present of £200 to her nephew Lt. Colonel Edward George Moore Donnithorne who married Harriette Lucia Alexander on 8 July 1875. Eliza's correspondent blames an *attack of your former ailment* on worries about *land taken from you for the purpose of making a public road and the small sum offered as compensation.* He begs her to return home as soon as she's well enough.

The NSW government, in charge of Newtown Road, refused to pay for the gas lamps and for a year the road was unlit. In 1877 it became King Street and was attaining its characteristic silhouette, still recognisable today, of handsome Victorian buildings.

By 1879 an upholsterer, gardener, baker and solicitor had set up businesses in Eliza's neighbourhood. Oddly, Miss Donnithorne was listed in the Sands directory for that year as *dressmaker*. Maybe it was her dressmaker who'd opened the door. That year Eliza received a visit from an associate of her advisor James Pratt, a Mr Bishop, to whom she gave a parcel for Pratt – a gold scarf pin with pearls – as well as presents for her relatives in England.

Eliza's popular image is wrapped in text and textiles, most suggestively the satin, silk and lace of the wedding dress she is supposed to have worn to shreds. Sexy ambiguities – games of interiority and exteriority – reside in the scaffolding and layering of lace. It's a flirtatious fabric. The critic Anne Kraatz says lace *succeeds in giving form to what is emptiness,* that it captures transparency; she sees the wearing of lace, throughout history, as an accentuation or *staging* of the self. Australian lace-maker and lace-historian Rosemary Shepherd believes the spaces are the most important element of lace, that *looking through a filter of spaces lends a different perspective to the view beyond.* Eliza now appears to us at some remove and through just such a complex screen.

In 1881 her correspondent thanked her for a postcard *with enchanted views of Sydney, which is evidently making wonderful progress.* The population of Newtown was 17,870, more than double that in 1871. Another girls' school, Camden College, was set up at the southern end of King Street. The suburb now had a new tramline. Royal Prince Alfred hospital opened, not far from Camperdown Lodge. Residents were tired of complaining about the dust and gathered 3,000 signatures petitioning to woodblock the road. In 1883 Eliza's neighbours Abram and Naomi Solomon held a *minyan* (Jewish prayer service) at their home in Georgina Street, close to the site where a synagogue would be built in 1918–19. In 1884 Camperdown Lodge became 36 King Street. Cabinet makers, stonemasons, blacksmiths and saddlers appeared nearby. Houses for sale were often advertised as being near Miss Donnithorne's house.

Eliza's half-sister Agnes Swetenham died in London in 1880. Her quarrelsome brother Edward Harris Donnithorne died in 1885; his widow Georgiana three years later. Edward Harris's son Colonel Edward George Moore Donnithorne inherited Colne Lodge. Rosamund Carnsew, now aged 20, who had continued to live at Colne Lodge with her grandparents, moved out. By 1891 she was living with her widowed father and half-sister Hilda in Herefordshire.

Edward junior moved into Colne Lodge with his family and seven servants. He was educated at Charterhouse and the Royal Military Academy at Woolwich, gazetted to the Scots Greys regiment; in New Zealand in April 1864 he was present at the storming of the Gate Pā and received a medal for his service. He must have been part of the first or second assault force that entered the *pā* after heavy bombardment, and a survivor of the close-range fighting. The battle was won by the Maori. He was also in Ireland to quell the Fenian insurrection. A document I've seen describes him as a *gallant soldier and an English gentleman*: it states that his grandfather James Donnithorne was Judge Chief Commisioner and Governor of the Bengal Mint and that he left two sons and three daughters. A Justice of the Peace, devoted to fairness and public matters, of unbiased mind and sound judgement, a staunch Conservative in politics, opposed to Tariff Reform, it said Edward believed in the future stability of the Empire; giving his London address as 76 Queen's Gate, Kensington.

Eliza Donnithorne died on 20 May 1886, just short of 65. The cause of death: disease of the lungs and heart, which (according to her death certificate) she'd been suffering for over twenty years. Two days later she was buried in Camperdown Cemetery, in her father's grave. Perhaps the dust had contributed to her illness; the woodblocking of King Street was not finished until 1891.

The first telephones were connected the year Eliza died;

eavesdropping on party lines was all the rage. By 1887 Camperdown Lodge was leased to Mrs Guy and in 1888 to Dr Murtagh, who renamed it Cambridge Hall and set up a school, an *Unsectarian Academy*. It failed. Murtagh auctioned his belongings, including a *magnificently built carriage, a barouche*. Joseph Murtagh presented himself as a Doctor of Philosophy from St Cuthbert's College in the North of England (also known as Ushaw College, a Catholic seminary linked to the University of Durham). He had already set up a school that failed the previous year, the Redfern Unsectarian College at 52 George Street, Redfern. There he'd been in partnership with Louisa Flatman, a widow, as housekeeper. And she did not pay the bills on time, so Mr Macnamara, a Redfern butcher, sued the doctor of philosophy for the sum of £9 14 shillings and 10 pence. The dispute went to court. By 1889, Murtagh was in Western Australia, and again in court, claiming *£7,000 damages for slanderous statements made on his private and public character at Coolgardie.* A Mr James Rigg, builder, had called Murtagh a scoundrel, *but did not remember suggesting that the plaintiff acted indecently towards some of the girls.* However, Rigg did not believe Murtagh was *a suitable man to be in charge of a school.* It was noted that Murtagh gave music lessons in his own room, where the piano stood in one corner, the bed in the other, and the door was shut; it was also noted that he *had the reputation of being fond of litigation.* Murtagh was awarded £250 damages. Coolgardie is really a long way from Eliza Donnithorne's story. But I do wonder if rumours associated with Cambridge Hall and Murtagh – from *St Cuthbert's* College – got muddled up with rumours about Eliza, and somehow the Chinese whispers of gossip produced the name of Eliza's runaway groom as Cuthbertson. That sort of thing does happen.

In July 1888 the property was subdivided as part of Kettle's Estate, much of it purchased by Samuel Hordern. The house continued to be known as Cambridge Hall (and it's around this time that Mary Gilmore appears to have been looking for Eliza, and imagining she found her).

A few years later, on the opposite side of King Street, the Trocadero – a *pleasure resort* – was built. Lit with electric lights, it included shops, dance hall, roller-skating rink, hairdresser, billiard and oyster saloons, rooms for smoking, reading and chess, and the Café Francaise, complete with fountain.

Newtown was the most significant retail centre outside the city. Real estate was booming. There were now a dozen brick factories in the area and Newtown's bricks were famous. Well supplied with transport options, by the late 1880s King Street (quoting from the *Illustrated Sydney News*, 27 June 1889) is *always more or less busy* and *on Saturday night*, when it *is at its best and brightest…more than a mile…of brilliantly lighted shops…the throng of people on business and pleasure bent…such a display of silks and satins, and ribbons and laces, and gloves and bonnets…plums and figs and teas and coffees…and lollipops and spices.* Not to mention second-hand books. People's thirst was quenched in nearly thirty hotels. The Palmer Buildings were erected on the corner of King and Queen, housing the Eastern Tea Company and a grocery store.

Eliza had been an independent woman in nineteenth-century Newtown, where other women – though mostly from a different social background – made a living as teachers and nurses, grocers, drapers, fortune-tellers, confectioners, milliners, newsagents, dressmakers and publicans. Of the more famous, Mary Reiby spent the last years of her entrepreneurial life in a house she built at 31 Station Street. And Ann Rumpf had cleverly used the mortgage on one property to finance another, and bought first the entire block of land between Forbes and Queen Streets, then several adjoining properties in King Street and elsewhere. Along King and Forbes Streets she established the Mount Eagle Tin Plate Metal Works.

In *Solitude – A Return to the Self*, Anthony Storr said of the reclusive Immanuel Kant that *although generous to his relatives, he took care to keep well away from them*. The same might be said of Eliza.

Eliza had property in England and Ireland. The executors of her British will were her nephews Edward George Moore Donnithorne and Arthur Bampton Donnithorne, and her niece's husband Edward Archer Wilde; these descendants, their children, and Rosamund Carnsew, were her heirs. She left money to her financial advisor James Boulton Pratt, to former *valued servants in my family* Mary Anne Cox and William Nicholas Cox, Grace Cox and Mary Fletcher, and to her cousin Agatha

Georgina Florence James (sister of Rev. Sir Vyell Donnithorne Vyvyan, Baronet of Treelowarren in Cornwall).

She bequeathed her father's organ to her late brother Edward Harris Donnithorne. She asked for her jewellery, books, drawings, engravings, china, glass and boxes of *fancy articles*, business letters and papers, likewise her *Indian and China Trunks and Boxes and... collection of curiosities to be sent to England*. She wanted her piano and harp to be sold. And she requested a new headstone for her *dearest Father's grave*, and to be buried in the same grave. She assigned £200 each to the diocese of Sydney and the British and Foreign Bible Society, £50 to the Society for Prevention of Cruelty to Animals, an annuity of £5 for each of her six animals and £5 for all her birds, for their keep *in the same state of comfort* as she had given them. We don't know what the six animals were, perhaps dogs, cats and horses. From the phrase *all my birds* I understand that there were many, that she may have kept a dovecote, or an aviary, a pair of peacocks, parrots that talked, canaries that sang. Or did she, like Dickens, have a pet raven? Because the Miss Havisham character is always represented amidst dead things, I like to think of Eliza surrounded by her menagerie of living and loved creatures and attending her collection of curiosities and books. *Every passion borders on the chaotic, but the collector's passion borders on the chaos of memories... there is in the life of a collector a dialectical tension between the poles of disorder and order* (Walter Benjamin, *Illuminations*).

She played the harp, a wondrous instrument. Perhaps she embroidered; we know from the correspondence that she sent a needlework purse to Chalmers. Or did she make lace, did she craft complex patterns of open and closed spaces, like a meditation? Perhaps her drawings were botanical, and her own work.

Eliza had employed about six servants, including other members of the Bailey family. My searches for them or their descendants, hoping they might have stories to tell, have been unsuccessful. There was a servant called Franz (later Frank) Adam Bibo. One of his descendants told me his family was French (originally de Bibon), but had settled as farmers in Nassau, Germany, near the Dutch border. Franz Bibo arrived with his mother and brothers on the *Chimborazo* at Port Melbourne in January 1881, when he was twenty-four. Late one night on the internet I find a watercolour of *The Chimborazo in Hobsons Bay*; I print it out and place it in my Bibo folder. It's said Franz spoke a dozen languages, with a reading knowledge of eight more. He continued his education in Australia; some of his family settled at Eastern Creek, Blacktown and Quaker's Hill, where they established vineyards. It's not known how long he worked for Eliza at Camperdown Lodge. In 1889 he married Elizabeth Kinnane in Sydney, and taught at a school in Wagra. I look for Wagra and find it was a small town in NSW, also called Wagragobilly, near Gundagai. This thread, interesting in itself, has not fetched any new information about Eliza.

All Eliza's servants received a legacy of £20. Her greatest generosity was shown to her servant Sarah Ann Bailey, who was named her executor and the main beneficiary of her estate in Australia, estimated at £12,000. The inventory of her deceased estate included her properties at 112 and 114 Victoria Road in Darlinghurst, valued at around £1,800 (a separate note describes this property as *very much out of repair*). About £100 in the Bank of Australasia. Money in the house: £277. Furniture and Effects £370. Shares in the Sydney Building and Investment Company £9,000 plus £135 interest. Money lent to Mr Edwin T. Sayers £500 plus interest (this is a big loan, perhaps it was some kind of investment; he was the son of Edwin Mawney Sayers, a shipowner and colourful Sydney personality who was renowned for rowing daily to the city from his home at Lavender Bay). Eliza also owned a section of the Undercliffe Estate in Sydney's inner-west. And she specified that her property in Victoria, Montmorency Estate, in the Parish of Nillumbik in the County of Evelyn, should continue to be leased out.

Sarah Ann Bailey had been instructed to distribute various legacies from the income from the sale of properties, also to pack up and send her late mistress's specified items back to England. She could then choose from the remaining household contents whatever *she may require for furnishing a cottage and cultivating and managing a garden,* which means Camperdown Lodge itself had substantial grounds that had required management. Everything else was sold on site.

On 12 October 1886 the *Sydney Morning Herald* announced the sale *At the Residence of the LATE MISS DONNITHORNE*, offering *the whole of the VALUABLE HOUSEHOLD FURNITURE, PLATE…HARP, best London make, PIANOFORTE, ditto…The furniture throughout is cedar and mahogany, of the best kind, BRASS BEDSTEADS and H.H. mattresses, secretaires, bookcases…wardrobes, telescope…*

I ask the Tasmanian harpmaker Andrew Thom if he thought Eliza's harp might still be in Australia, and receive an unequivocal *no*. He tells me harps have a short working life, about twenty five years, there's too much tension in them, they *tear themselves apart*, they warp and twist and *fall to pieces*. But he suggests, to be sure, I should ask the academic and one of the world's leading harp soloists, Alice Giles; she says there are still plenty of old harps around but *most would not be playable*, and suggests Eliza's was probably made by a company called Erard.

The historian Chrys Meader comes from a long line of Newtown residents. She tells me about her great-great-grandmother Catherine Fletcher, who *bought furniture at the auction of Miss Donnithorne's estate*, and that her Nana, who'd been told stories about Eliza, *always wanted to see her house, so when it was about to be demolished she decided to take a look and climbed the fence*. This was in the early 1900s, when Chrys's Nana May – Ethel May Clarke – was about sixteen, and one of her uncles, James Fletcher, lived in Queen Street. One of the stories passed on to Meader, was that Eliza did not wear white, on the contrary, she loved colours, especially shades of lavender and lilac. And that she had dark hair. Meader remembers:

Before her marriage in 1909 my Nana was a tailoress in Newtown. She was told by an old woman who had been a seamstress in a city dressmaking firm that Eliza Emily Donnithorne had clothes made and altered once a year at Camperdown Lodge. She was never measured but was seen. One of the head dressmakers would go to Camperdown Lodge and be given material – she mentioned bales of Indian silk in beautiful colours. She also mentioned the indoor and outdoor aviaries. My impression from these childhood stories was that Camperdown Lodge was not quite the dismal, gloomy place that Satis House was in the book. Eliza had a liking for exotic colours and objects in her surroundings. I love this anecdote, because it completely contradicts the notion of Eliza's abstinence from worldly pleasures and kicks over the *jilted spinster* stereotype.

In taking care of the deceased estate, in August 1886 Sarah Ann Bailey also had to pay Eliza's debts: to the wine merchants Burne & Co, to Mr Maddock for a book, to the local cabinet maker Mr (Henrick Louis) Metzler, to the legal firm Gurner & Robberds of 33 George Street, and the newsagent West for delivery of newspapers. Was Metzler making another cabinet for her curiosities?

About 1895–98 Camperdown Lodge, now Cambridge Hall, was occupied by the Engisch family. George Engisch was an advertising agent and the only full photo known to exist of the house is probably from that period…it shows billboards attached to the picket fence, and the house no longer set back from the road, which must have been widened; there's a single Norfolk Island pine left standing; in front, two small children, and a horse and carriage. The house was demolished a few years later. What went up in its place? In August 1915 newspapers reported *A Mysterious Fire* (the second in a few years) on the block bounded by King, Georgina and Fitzroy streets, that turned the Newtown Stadium, including a drill hall containing 1,000 rifles, ammunition and uniforms, into *a smoking heap of debris*. But the managing director of the Stadium Company *did not think the fire had been started by the anti-boxing element, particularly as the building had been largely used by patriotic efforts*.

With their inheritance, the Bailey sisters had enough money to buy a house at 63 Lennox Street, Newtown, not far from Eliza's grave; Sarah Ann died there in 1912, aged eighty-three. Their brother Walter Bailey married Elizabeth Ferguson in Newtown in 1886; their niece Mary Bailey lived at 32 Rose Street, Chippendale.

Eliza also left an annuity of £20 to Mrs Jones. Ann Kelly Jones had been living nearby, her last address was 44 College Street, Camperdown. She died aged 80 in October 1897.

Ann's son with James Donnithorne – and therefore Eliza's half-brother – was known as James Kelly Donithorne Jones. A customs officer, he married Elizabeth Amelia Selby in 1864 and they lived in

Chippendale and Redfern. Their children were Elizabeth Emily Kelly, born 1865, Isabella Beatrice Kelly, 1866, Maude Jones, 1870, Ernest Jones, 1873, Arthur Montague Jones, 1875, twins Florence and Claude Jones, 1882, and Valetta Jones, 1886. Carol Moeser, the granddaughter of Arthur Montague Jones – thus the great-great-granddaughter of James Donnithorne – tells me that in her family her great-grandmother Elizabeth Selby was remembered as a very dignified, *strong, generous lady always dressed in black taffeta with lace collars* and that *her table was always laid with the best silver and cut glass*. James K. D. Jones was also in a de facto relationship with Elizabeth Mansfield and they had two children, James (called Prince) Jones (1897), and Annie (1886), who later had a newspaper stand at Parramatta station. He died in 1918 in Parramatta, aged 78. The children of both households were well acquainted with each other.

One of Ann's descendants, her granddaughter Isabella's daughter, was Vera Fernance. I've read that John Fernance, a *waterman on the Thames*, had been convicted of *piracy* for stealing thirteen lumps of sugar, sentenced to hang, but he was instead transported for life. His descendants then did well enough to have their sugar imported from England. Vera had been afraid of the water as a child and learned to swim when she was 64; she was still swimming twice a week well into her 90s and was a world-record holder for that age group. Also an accomplished violinist and pianist, she died aged 95 in 1993. As one of the custodians of family lore, she passed her stories and newspaper cuttings on to her relatives and descendants.

Of Eliza's heirs in England, Henrietta Maria's daughter Rosamund Carnsew married George Sabine. I've been told she belonged to the Society for Psychical Research (where the poet W.B. Yeats, psychologist C.G. Jung, and philosopher William James were also members) and have read she was associated with the magical order of the Golden Dawn and as *Old Mother Sabine*, it's possible she was a high priestess of the New Forest Coven of Neopagan witches, also called Wiccans. In the 1920s the Sabines lived at Highcliffe in Dorset, in the vicinity of two women also associated with witchcraft, Katherine Oldmeadow and the elusive *Old Dorothy* Clutterbuck (aka Dorothy Fordham), where during World War II they were members of the Home Guard, using magical powers to stop Hitler's troops from crossing the Channel. One of my correspondents, a researcher of witchcraft genealogies, points out the strong Donnithorne-Moore-Bevan-Carnsew families' connections with religion in Devon, Sussex and Cornwall, and wonders if there's not another *hidden stream* of a more pagan kind, which Rosamund inherited, or which attracted her. Rosamund died in 1948. According to a fellow Wiccan, she left a *nice little cabinet* of herbs, and a 1684 edition of Nicholas Culpeper's herbal.

It's an intriguing turn of the narrative. Miss Havisham at Satis House was described by Dickens as looking like *the witch of the place*. And in an episode of the cartoon *South Park* based on *Great Expectations*, Miss Havisham commands an army of monkeys, like the wicked witch in *The Wizard of Oz*. Shakespeare's Kate in *The Taming of the Shrew* describes spinsterhood as a terrible fate, that it was like *leading apes in hell.* In *A Room of One's Own*, Virginia Woolf wrote that when *one reads of a witch being ducked, of a woman possessed by devils, of a wise woman selling herbs, or even of a very remarkable man who had a mother, then I think we are on the track of a lost novelist, a suppressed poet, of some mute or inglorious Jane Austen, some Emily Brontë who dashed her brains out on the moor or mopped and mowed about the highways crazed with the torture that her gift had put her to.* Woolf imagines *Shakespeare's sister ended her days in some lonely cottage outside the village, half witch, half wizard, feared and mocked at.* I was pleased to have found Rosamund – Eliza's great-niece and heir – as Old Mother Sabine. I now had two enigmatic women, closely related, who chose to live outside society.

In the early 1900s Eliza's niece Mary Penelope, whose husband Edward Archer Wilde had died in 1889, lived in London. They had seven children, two boys who died in infancy, one son Arthur who married his first cousin Guinevere Cicely Arundell Donnithorne (daughter of Arthur Bampton Donnithorne) and four daughters: Mary, Elizabeth, Henrietta and Violet. It's thought at least two of them remained unmarried and continued to live with their mother. A Donnithorne descendant tells me that as a young girl her mother had heard that her *unwed older Wilde cousins were very clever, eccentric, well read and rather daunting*. I like to think that they inherited some of their great aunt Eliza's books. I haven't been able to find out much about Mary Penelope, only that she was a member of the Royal Horticultural Society, so I see her growing magnificent orchids with great success on a deep warm windowsill at 84 Lexham Gardens, Kensington. I know she liked cooking. She continued to add recipes to the notebook she had begun as a young woman in 1862. It shows a fondness for desserts, gooseberry wine and ginger beer, and contains a few Anglo-Indian dishes. I'm intrigued by something called Country Captain, which requires quite a lot of chillies. I google it and find the *New York Times* recently featured it and called it a one-pot wonder. Mary Penelope's notebook still has her old blotting papers. There are also recipes on odd scraps of paper, and newspaper cut-outs, unsorted, slid between the front and back covers of the notebook. The Census of 1911 shows Rosamund Carnsew aged 46, visiting her aunt Mary Wild and cousin Henrietta, who were looked after by five servants. Mary Penelope died in 1918, but the dates of some recipe cuttings are as late as 1944, and carry the initials E.M.W., so Mary's daughter Elizabeth must have inherited the cookbook and continued the collection. On the reverse of *One set of recipes for Five delicious dishes from one packet of dried eggs* – war rations – there's a report of *Montgomery's spearheads…only eight miles from the Rhine big bridge town of Emmerich*: it refers to 7 October

1944 when allied bombing destroyed most of the town of Emmerich on the German-Dutch border.

Eliza's nephew Edward and his family moved into Colne Lodge. He was the inventor of a kind of razor wire used extensively in warfare and an early pioneer of the motor industry in England; at Twickenham he established the Colne Valley Engineering Company, which ran for about five years but closed in 1894; he also experimented with the development of automatic rifles. There were five children, Harold Edward Alexander Comyn, Lilian Loveday Emily, Loveday Isabel, Vyvyan Henry, and in 1889, Edith Harriette. She told her story to her daughter Faith, who wrote it down for her daughter Judith: the French governess until she was five, the large garden with an icehouse and a stream at one end, and how things changed in about 1894 because, she believed, her father had lost his money – indeed, he'd used up his wife's dowry – trying to patent an automatic rifle. He had to resign from the army, and to leave Colne Lodge in 1897. They bought a cottage in Twickenham. *Edward took to laudanum to ease his sufferings*. To earn money his wife started a laundry which her son Harold helped to run, *a thing no gentleman had ever done, but it did well.* Edward died 19 November 1906; the house was demolished in 1913. Harriette rented a flat in Queen's Gate, London. When Eliza's legacy came through – she'd left £1,000 to her nephews and nieces – *Harold used his exploring x rays, Vyvyan put himself through Cambridge University, while Lilian and Loveday pooled their money to run a hatshop in London which failed*; and they got married. In fact all of Edith's siblings married four siblings called Ingram. Edith's inheritance helped her mother pay the rent and move to a cottage in Wimbledon *where she was very happy*. Harriette died in 1935.

Eliza's nephew Arthur Bampton and his wife Aeddan Arundell had a son called Clarence Edward Stuart Comyn Donnithorne (a missionary in India and Burma, and a freemason), who married Winifred Strickland Taylor (descended from Samuel Strickland, brother of the nineteenth-century Canadian authors Susanna Moodie, Catherine Parr Traill and Agnes Strickland). Their son Ralph Donnithorne, born 1912, was a great collector of books and art works and in later life was a neighbour and friend of the poet T.S. Eliot; according to Ralph's daughter, both of them were *quiet* men.

Of Eliza's contemporaries, Marianne Shakespear – whose mother was heartbroken when her little girl was sent to England – married Major J. Irvine of the Bengal Engineers; she died in 1891. Marianne's sister Selina Shakespear, born just before Eliza in the Donnithorne's house in Capetown, lived until 1908. She never married. Her relative, the memoirist Ursula Low, recalled *her upright carriage, snowy hair and delicate pink and white complexion.*

What Remains

On the internet I've seen an eight-volume set of *The Works of Shakespeare* offered for sale; published 1747, with critical notes by Mr Pope and Mr Warburton – rebacked spines...leather brittle...some corners worn... some pages toned – it comes with the *near-contemporary signature of 'George Moore, Sowton'*, and a small *attractive stamp* depicting a bird of E.H. Donnithorne. Perhaps Eliza owned similar kinds of books.

Some paintings. The one of Nicholas Donnithorne is on loan to St Agnes Museum. In private possession there's a painting of Eliza's two sisters Maria and Penelope as young girls. The younger one has been incorrectly identified by Godl as Eliza. There's a painting in the same naive style, of Eliza's brothers William and Edward and a dog. As children, all four siblings were fair-haired with a hint of red.

Some miscellaneous memories. Colin Harris, who lives in St Agnes, Cornwall, tells me one of the current county councillors is a Donnithorne, but that the original family is *essentially forgotten*. He remembers that before the World War there were some Donnithornes who made fizzy drinks in *bottles with a marble in the neck*.

The cookbook. If Eliza swapped recipes with her niece Mary Penelope, or had inherited similar ones, then as I peep through the window at Camperdown Lodge, instead of the grotesque remains of Miss Havisham's never-eaten wedding breakfast – or the figure conjured by Randolph Stow, *here comes the bride, stark mad in white satin. And her maid, stark sane in black bombazine, and with such a pretty apron* – I see a charming household scene, some glistening Syrup and Sago moulds, or a set of perfect Prince Albert Puddings, and a jug of homemade ginger beer, freshly laid out on a sunny kitchen table, because Mrs Jones is coming for morning tea.

The memory of lace. The economist Audrey Donnithorne remembers her father Vyvyan Henry Donnithorne telling her *when he was very young, his father received some lace from a deceased relative in Australia*, but her father *did not know who this relative was*. The family no longer has this lace. Was it Eliza's? An anti-macassar depicting an allegorical scene? Napkins or a doily? Or something she'd worn, a gown or stole or veil, cuffs or a collar?

The gravestone. Some articles suggest – incorrectly – that Eliza died on the same day in May as her father, as if her strongest attachment had always been to him. I've made inquiries and was told that for lack of space it was quite common for family members to be buried in the same grave. The inscription reads: *In Memory of James Donnithorne Esq For Many Years Governor of the Mint And a Judge in the Honourable East India Company Bengal Civil Service Died 25th May 1852 Aged 79 Years/ Also of Eliza Emily Donnithorne Last Surviving Daughter of the Above Died 20 May 1886*. The phrase *last surviving daughter* is very moving, a tribute to her sisters, who did not survive.

And so James is remembered as a *Judge*, just as Leichhardt was a *Doctor* and Strzelecki was a *Count*. You could arrive here and notch up your social status without too many questions.

The Moreton Bay Fig and the old oaks that grow in Camperdown Cemetery were planted in 1848. It's estimated that 18,000 people were buried there, including those drowned on the Dunbar in 1857, Napoleon's harpist the composer and *escroc* Nicolas-Charles Bochsa, the explorer Thomas Livingstone Mitchell, members of the Macleay family, Thomas Downes who was killed in a balloon accident in the Domain in 1856, and Frank Huxham, killed by a bull in Castlereagh Street in 1854. The cemetery has a history of being vandalised, dates for these destructions include 1934, 1950, 1954, 1975, 1976, 1978. In November 2004 the Donnithornes' grave was desecrated, its marble headstone broken. Donations from the Dickens society – and as one paper reported, a massive community effort, dog walkers, the gothic community and local residents – ensured the restoration. Regarding the incident, the Rev. Peter Rodgers of St Stephen's Church thought *a group got drunk and took great delight in destroying a grave… they were picking on a single grave and it just happens to be under a grove of trees; it's a nice spot to sit.*

Back on the Corner of King and Queen

Today someone living in self-imposed social isolation might be diagnosed as suffering ochlophobia (also called demophobia) – a fear of crowds – or Avoidant Personality Disorder, for which there are therapies and drugs. The modern recluse can also shop around, for blogs, dwellings, holidays. On the internet someone asks why some people choose to be reclusive. One answer: *to escape drama*. Another: *DUUUUUUDDDE! have you seen the world?* I recently found a website called *reclusivity.net* offering various assistance for reclusion: a prefabricated room which can be constructed away from the main house, a chest of drawers *supported from within* called Introvert, a comment from *Phantom of the Opera* actor Gerard Butler who said I *know I have within myself…a side of solitude…I can seriously go into my own head*, and something eighteenth- and nineteenth-century heroines of Gothic novels should have had, a doorknob that can be pulled towards the inside of the room to become *a guardian of anonymity, the keeper of a secret moment* – as well as remote Bishop Rock in the Atlantic, once a place where criminals were left to die alone, now *up to four visitors can stay there for one to three weeks*. Appropriately, *reclusivity.net* has now become a *dropped domain* and is no longer available.

My own early assignations with solitude were weighed with guilt. Too often reclusion is a social taboo. You're called a leper, a quitter, an idler, a weirdo, a grump, it's thought you have something to hide. Because social cohesion is a fragile construct that's easily undone, we're taught to uphold it by every possible means, through appropriate body language and respect for cultural and familial kinships, and increasingly, a sense of global responsibility. We're sustained by communalities and we expect – we are expected – to live companionably and more or less collectively. We question our affiliations only when they become treacherous, or superfluous.

Affable types – garrulous, cheerful, busily hobnobbing, team playing – don't really get it: that for some people self-exile is desirable, part necessity, part pleasure, it's the fork in the road considered, and taken. It's not something for which one seeks redemption, nor is it necessarily an extreme mental state. The stigma of madness – especially in literature – gives solitude a bad name. Many agendas of institutional sociability take advantage of our fears. In a BBC series *The Case for God?* (2010), Rabbi Jonathan Sacks said that *religion is the redemption of solitude*, a comment echoed by other religious leaders. This kind of reasoning plays emotional tricks on us and disavows the human need for withdrawal.

Dickens, his biographers tell us, was boundlessly sociable. From the very beginning of his career his popularity became an extraordinary literary phenomenon. His relationship with his reading public has been compared to a love-affair. Like his characters, he needed a crowd, or at the very least, constant companionship. But I suspect inside Dickens the crowd-man and family-man, inside his work, is a hidden source, a kernel, a Pip who is drawn instinctively – and much to his own horror – to the solitude of Miss Havisham. Both he and she have been abandoned, she jilted, he orphaned. A child's most fantasised what-if is the idea of being without parents and imagining how one gets on in the world alone. *Great Expectations*, starting with a child visiting his parents' graves, is a book of orphans and surrogacy. Orphanhood – abandonment – is Dickens' specialty, linked to a solitary self, his secret, suppressed, mummified, gothicised, narrated, complicated, made suspenseful, *expectant*, his own inner *Miss Havisham*. In nineteenth- and twentieth-century literature, abandonment finds expression not just in stories of victimhood – lovers jilted, children left by parents – but also actively, as rebellion and the breaking free from gender expectations or an autocratic older generation. It's a dominant theme closely linked to ideas of reclusion in the work of Franz Kafka, for example.

In the story 'The Burrow' Kafka wrote (in the guise of a mole-like creature), *I have completed the construction of my burrow and it seems to be successful. All that can be seen from the outside is a big hole; that, however, really leads nowhere; if you take a few steps you strike against natural firm rock.* The hole is a ruse. *But you do not know me if you think I am afraid, or that I built my burrow simply out of fear.* The real entrance to the burrow is nearby. Inside, the burrower is both safe from and vulnerable to intrusion: he mentions robbers and an itinerant beast, but his greatest enemy is noise. He acts awkwardly. He is rather too much preoccupied with defensive measures and modifications. But a few moments of *the sheer pleasure of the mind in its own keenness*, of living *in peace in the inmost chamber of my house*, of losing himself in his own maze, and the stillness there, make it all worthwhile. He knows *all the passages and how they run*, and is *connected with the outer world by quite narrow, tolerably safe passages*. While the burrow is the product of intense intellectual labour, the chief cell – the Castle Keep – is the result of *the most arduous labour of my whole body*. It's there he piles up his stores, and where he sleeps most deeply and is most keenly awake. He worries about the wisdom of keeping everything in one place. Sometimes he flees the burrow. Then returns from his wanderings. Sometimes he digs experimental burrows, which he decides are useful *as a further means of ventilation*. Needless to say 'The Burrow' – a meditation on self burial, or self-birthing – is an unfinished story. The reader is an intruder who can't know how it ends.

Gaston Bachelard, the postmaster who became a philosophy professor interested in psychology – but who remained modest, with a *marked provincial accent* – associates the contentment of withdrawal with our very first, primitive and intensely physical sense of huddling or hiding. In *The Poetics of Space*, his collection of interiorities – houses, huts, wardrobes, nests, shells, snow, boxes, corners, miniatures – are *protected intimacies* and *states of emergence* and *felicitous* spaces, which are rarely melancholic. Reading Bachelard always makes me want to puff up the cushions, and put fresh flowers in a vase. Psychologically, he is interested in reserve, defined for instance by the kinds of moods that will make children *leave a game to go and be bored in a corner of the garret.* Philosophically, he explores the dialectics of outside and inside, the ways in which the universe comes to inhabit intimate spaces, like a house.

Similarly, the humanist philosopher Michel de Montaigne, in his essay *On Solitude*, feels goodness and wisdom are within reach if we know how to *keep a little room at the back of the shop, all our own and entirely free*, a place to experience our essential solitude. In 1571 he retired to the library in the tower of his ancestral castle in southwest France, and tried to live in reclusion until his death in 1592, a plan interrupted by illness, travel and civic responsibilities. Like Montaigne, people inclined to seek reclusion often also remain socially engaged. The American individualist, and advocate of simple living, Henry David Thoreau, wrote in an essay titled 'Visitors', I *had three chairs in my house, one for solitude, two for friendship, three for society.*

While some forms of voluntary exile are humoured, as in the cubbies or tree houses of childhood, or the garden shed, or are valued as a way to higher understanding, the spiritual retreat, still the force of communality is so strong, so much threatened by individuality and reclusion, that we are inclined sooner or later and somehow to return to the fold. Jacques Lacan explains it as the I always being in the field of the Other. Even hermit saints are not alone forever, placed as they are within populous scriptural narratives, or as founders of movements. Sometimes solitude is tentative, or comes in couples, or small, scattered groups, like the desert monastic communities of the third century. Wordsworth rarely wandered too far from his cottage or from the women there who baked pies for him. I asked a philosopher how Heidegger coped; he thought Frau Elfride Heidegger was always nearby, boiling up cabbage soup. And Wittgenstein in his hideout on Lake Eidsvatnet in Norway? No need for a cook. He was easy to please, being fond of undemanding food like rye bread and cheese; he is supposed to have said I *don't care what I eat so long as it is always the same.*

Samuel Beckett liked to walk, and read, hated chatter, loved silence. Probably he did not watch his diet; in his reclusion he was plagued with bad health: boils, cysts and palpitations.

Emily Dickinson, *connaisseuse* of solitudes whose *Soul selects her own society – Then – shuts the Door*, knew well that anything at all – compassion, fear, summer, or a fly – will enter to claim her company.

In *A Room of One's Own* Virginia Woolf equated privacy with personal freedom and throughout her life created for herself an uneasy balance of seclusion and sociability. Mostly, she did not mind being alone, but feared loneliness. She stressed the importance of choice and thought *how unpleasant it is to be locked out; and...how it is worse perhaps to be locked in*. These anxieties – of expulsion and confinement – have been a literary mainspring throughout history, with an increase of attention from the eighteenth century to the present. It is a Gothic obsession. One of the most visceral examples of the fear of being locked in, and not finding an exit, is 'The Iron Shroud' (1830), a short story by William Mudford, complete with disappearing windows and contracting walls and ceiling. A century later, the oppressed characters of Jean-Paul Sartre's play *Huis Clos* (1944) become their own means of entrapment.

Since childhood, when his father was sent to Marshalsea debtors' prison, Dickens had a horror of and fascination with prisons. He never got over it; all his life he wrote about the penal system and campaigned for reforms. In his essay 'Where we stopped growing', he describes prisons, and the sight of the White Woman of Berner's Street, as two pivotal experiences which arrested his development, an extraordinary idea when he seemed in all other ways unstoppable. When he wasn't working, he was walking. Like Woolf, Dickens found his own safe degree of solitude in the crowded streets of London. The Woolfian ideal was to be *thinking about unusual things* while rambling. The solitary walker – alone in Nature, or Baudelairean, in a crowd – is a much-rehearsed Romantic figure.

Some writers seek reclusion, but are not at ease with it. Some make a fetish of the melancholy associated with being alone. Sebald in Suffolk, in *Rings of Saturn*, feels at once *utterly liberated and deeply despondent*, uncertain *whether walking in this solitary way was more of a pleasure or a pain*. Critics have noted that his solitudes are in fact *extravagantly peopled* with outsiders, bachelors and spinsters, eccentrics, exiles, and the dead. He wrote, it's the *ghosts of repetition that haunt me*. Sebald's *characters*, even his water-beetle rowing from one side of a rain barrel to the other, back and forth, are incarnations of Wittgenstein's iconic image of interiority: the idea that every person has his or her own *beetle in a box*.

In Nietzschean terms, reclusion treads a knife-edge between good and evil. Close by, Martin Heidegger said what he felt in his hut at Todtnauberg in the Black Forest was not loneliness but solitude, which *has the peculiar and original power of not isolating us but projecting our whole existence out into the vast nearness of the presence of all things*. That's fine, I say, as long as the *vast nearness* of the *Heimatland* doesn't also reside and fester in the hut; as long as the Romantic concept doesn't harbour a Nationalist fetish to lock some people out, or lock them up, or worse.

The writers and philosophers who explore personal boundaries and solitudes, including the private and liminal nature of language – Dickinson, Heidegger, Woolf, the Austrian writer Ingeborg Bachmann, Australian Gerald Murnane, Americans Djuna Barnes, Harper Lee, May Sarton and Willa Cather, Thomas Pynchon and J.D. Salinger, the

British novelist Anna Kavan, and further back, mystics like Hildegard of Bingen – they're all Miss Havishams. They turn and go. And their retreat offends and fascinates us. How dare they? Why do they? Like Orpheus marching into Hades to fetch his runaway bride, we grab at their shadows. We can't stand their absence and autonomy and must seek them out, gather them in like orphans, second-guess their secrets and measure the truth of it all. Like the comedian and traveller Michael Palin, who became intrigued by the reclusive Danish artist Vilhelm Hammershøi and in a documentary tried *to find out everything I can about this man, whose work caught my imagination and has never let it go*. Hammershøi painted spare interiors in muted shades, with light from doors and windows. Many are empty, some include Orphic backviews of his wife Ida. In his search for *the secret* about Hammershøi, Michael Palin speculates that Ida may have inherited *mental health problems* from her mother, and taking a closer look at the least flattering of Ida's portraits, he thinks he sees a *troubled soul* and wonders if she was the reason that Hammershøi didn't have a social life.

Women are universally linked with interiority and literary scholars have suggested that Miss Havisham's alienation is typical of hysterical insanity. Nineteenth-century physicians identified hysteria as a psychosomatic womb-related disease, particularly of middle-class women, and put its tag on a wide range of symptoms, including headaches, depression, pain, paralysis, seizures, sexual excess or frigidity.

The reclusive American poet Emily Dickinson – whose lifespan 1830 to 1886 matched Eliza's and who had a predilection for white dresses – was placed into this roomy category, though it's now believed she actually suffered from epilepsy, and this was the taboo that kept her cloistered.

So far it's not been possible to establish what, if anything, was wrong with Eliza. She seems to have been laid low by an unnamed chronic illness – physical or mental, or both – which prevented her from returning to England, and which might also have been the reason for her reclusion. Or, having endured long journeys between India, England and Australia, she simply wanted to stay in one place, and used illness as an excuse to do so. Similarly, if the prospect of marriage was unappealing, with too much suffering associated with childbirth and motherhood, and she was nonetheless encouraged to marry, she may have invented a façade of illness and eccentricity as protection against these expectations. Women, including Florence Nightingale, another of Strachey's Eminent Victorians, were sometimes forced to use illness – real or affected – to gain a kind of independence. (And an unexpected connection: *It has never before been published that there was a romance deciding the going of Miss Florence Nightingale to the Crimea. She and James Arkwright were lovers, but the old squire, her father, opposed the union on the ground of class…Squire Nightingale is supposed to be the prototype of George Eliot's Squire Donnithorne in 'Adam Bede'. Hobart Mercury*, 1927.)

Eliza may have been seen as an hysteric, and her withdrawal from society as a form of self-punishment, a variation of the era's madwoman-in-the-attic phenomenon. If she reminds us of a mythological Medea or Penelope or a fairy-tale Rapunzel, Shakespeare's Ophelia or Tennyson's Lady of Shalott, they're also too extreme, none of them quite fit the portrait, Eliza's footprint was much lighter. Camperdown Lodge was not Satis House nor the Castle of Otranto nor Dickinson's alabaster chamber nor the cabin at Walden Pond. I suspect Eliza was no passion-driven-but-disappointed heroine. She was no transcendentalist, no Symeon of Trier, nor a poet, philosopher or artist. Her retreat from public life appears to have had no aesthetic, ascetic, didactic or epiphanic dimension. But as a reader she may have been well versed in literary examples of all these paradigms. We don't know what books she owned, but I imagine she agreed with the essayist Ralph Waldo Emerson, that I *am not solitary whilst I read and write, though nobody is with me.*

A SELECTION OF SOURCES

In *The Recluse*, quotations from other texts are in italics. My sources include personal conversations and correspondence, which remain private. In the course of my research I have gathered more material than I have incorporated in this biographical essay. I welcome comments, corrections and further information.

Reclusion and Literature

Nina Auerbach, *Woman and the Demon: The Life of a Victorian Myth* (1982); Gaston Bachelard, *The Poetics of Space* (1964); Jean Baudrillard, 'The System of Collecting', in John Elsner and Roger Cardinal, *The Cultures of Collecting* (1994); Walter Benjamin, *Illuminations* (1969); Charlotte Brontë, *The Professor* (1857); Charles Dickens, *Great Expectations* (1861), and 'Where we stopped growing', *Household Words*, 1.1.1853, vol VI. no 145, pp. 362–363, and supplement to *Household Words*, 1850; Emily Dickinson, *The Complete Poems of Emily Dickinson* (1890, edited by Thomas H. Johnson); Brian Dillon, *Tormented Hope: Nine Hypochondriac Lives* (2009); Wendy Doniger, *The Woman Who Pretended to Be Who She Was* (2005); George Eliot, *Adam Bede* (1859); Ralph Waldo Emerson, *Nature and Selected Essays* (1982); Michel Foucault, *History of Madness* (2006); Maryanne Garbowsky, *The House without the Door: a study of Emily Dickinson and the illness of agoraphobia* (1989); Ernest Gellner, *Language and Solitude* (1998); Sandra M. Gilbert and Susan Gubar, *The Madwoman in the Attic* (1979); Lyndall Gordon, *Lives Like Loaded Guns* (2010); Laurie Hergenhan, 'Mindscapes of the artist – visiting Randolph Stow', *ABR*, July–August 2010; Philip Heselton, *Gerald Gardner and the Cauldron of Inspiration* (2003); Christopher Hibbert, *Queen Victoria in her Letters and Journals* (1984); Michael Howard, *Modern Wicca – A History from Gerald Gardner to the Present* (2009); Sheila Jeffries, *The Spinster and Her Enemies* (1985); Susan Juhasz, *The Undiscovered Continent: Emily Dickinson and the Space of the Mind* (1983); Franz Kafka, 'The Burrow' ('Der Bau', 1931), in *Metamorphosis and Other Stories* (1961); Susan

Koppelman (ed), *Old Maids* (1984); Anne Kraatz, 'Lace, or the capturing of tranparency', *Textile Forum*, 1 (1997), pp. 46–47; Dietmar Laue, 'Lace and other airy things', *Textile Forum*, 3 (2010), pp. 24–25; Suzanne Marrs, *Eudora Welty: A Biography* (2006); Arnold H. Modell, *The Private Self* (1993); Michel de Montaigne, *The Complete Essays* (1991, translation M.A. Screech); Erica Obey, *The* Wunderkammer *of Lady Charlotte Guest* (2007); Keith Perry, 'Pining for lost love can be physically addictive', *The Telegraph* (UK) 28.6.2008; Marilynne Robinson, *Absence of Mind: The Dispelling of Inwardness from the Modern Myth of the Self* (2010); Jocelyn Rodal, 'One World, One Life': The politics of personal connection in Virginia Woolf's *The Waves* (MIT thesis, 2006); Hazel Rowley, *Christina Stead – A Biography* (2007); W.G. Sebald, *The Rings of Saturn* (1998); Adam Sharr, *Heidegger's Hut* (2006); Elaine Showalter, *The Female Malady* (1985); Michael Slater, *Dickens and Women* (1982) and *Charles Dickens* (2009); Barry Stone, I *Want To Be Alone* (2010); Anthony Storr, *Solitude – A Return to the Self* (1988); Lytton Strachey, *Eminent Victorians* (1918); Henry David Thoreau, *Walden* (1854), *Life in the Woods – Essays and Belles-Lettres* (1908); Claire Tomalin, *Charles Dickens – A Life* (2011); Patrick White, *Voss* (1957); Ludwig Wittgenstein, *Philosophical Investigations* (1953); Virginia Woolf, *Night and Day* (1919), *Orlando* (1928), *A Room of One's Own* (1929), *The Waves* (1931); *www.squalorsurvivors.com*

England

Anonymous, *Middlesex: biographical and pictorial* (1906); John Burke and Sir Bernard Burke, *A genealogical and heraldic history of the extinct and dormant baronetcies of England* (1741); Jane Carson, 'Lady Dunmore in Virginia', (1962) Research Department, Colonial Williamsburg Foundation, Williamsburg, Virginia; Mary Delaney (ed Augusta Hall), *Autobiography and Correspondence of Mary Granville, Mrs Delaney*, Vol 5 (1862, 2011); Isobel Grundy, *Lady Mary Wortley Montagu* (2001); Holger Hoock, *Empires of the Imagination – Politics, War, and the Arts in the British World, 1750–1850* (2010); Robert Hunt, Popular Romances of the West of England (1865); Evelyn Lord, *The Hellfire Clubs*

(2008); Lady Virginia Murray and Her Alleged Claim Against the State of Virginia, *The William and Mary Quarterly*, Vol. 24, No. 2 (Oct., 1915), pp. 85–101, Institute of Early American History and Culture; Donald Simpson, *Twickenham Past* (1993); Hallam Tennyson, *Alfred Lord Tennyson: A Memoir* (1897); Horace Walpole, *The Castle of Otranto* (1765); Paul Whitehead, Edward Thompson, *The poems and miscellaneous compositions of Paul Whitehead* (1777). Also: National Archives (Kew) Catalogue: Item ref HO 42/34/110 Folios 252–256; *The London Gazette*, 21 January, 1887; *The Solicitors' Journal and Reporter*, 1871; *www.twickenham-museum.org.uk*; *www.british-history.ac.uk*

India

C. Graham Botha's *Collected Works* (1883), vol 3, pp. 273, 277; Alison Blunt, 'Embodying war: British women and domestic defilement in the Indian *Mutiny*, 1857–8, *Journal of Historical Geography*, 26, 3, (2000) pp. 403–428; Douglas Dewar, *Bygone Days in India* (1875); Edward Dodwell, James Samuel Miles, *Alphabetical List of the honourable East Asia Company's Bengal Civil Servants*, pp. 142–145; E.M. Forster, *A Passage to India* (1924); Marquess of Hastings, *The Private Journal of the Marquess of Hastings* (1858); Edward Ingram (ed), *Two Views of British India – The Private Correspondence of Mr Dundas and Lord Wellesley: 1798–1801* (1969); Ursula Low, *Fifty Years with John Company: From the Letters of General Sir John Low of Clatto, Fife 1822–1858* (1936); Karl Marx, 'The East India Company – its History and Results', *New-York Herald Tribune* 24 June, 1853, p148; Mrs Meer Hasan Ali, *Observations on the Mussulmauns of India* (1832); Barbara D. Metcalf and Thomas R. Metcalf, *A Concise History of India* (2002); John Pester, *War and Sport in India 1802–1806 – an officer's diary* (1913); T.S. Randhawa, *The Sikhs – Images of a Heritage* (2000); Emma Roberts, *Scenes and Characteristics of Hindostan – with sketches of Anglo-Indian Society*, vol 3 (1835); Jane Robinson, *Angels of Albion* (1996); Klaus Stierstorfer (ed), *Women Writing Home, 1700–1920 – Female Correspondence across the British Empire, vol 4: India* (2006); Romila Thapar, *A History of India*, Vol I (1966), and Percival Spear, *A History of India*, Vol 2 (1956); C.L. Wallace, *Fatehgarh Camp 1777–1857* (1858);

T.F. Wilson and Saul David, *The Defence of Lucknow: T.F. Wilson's memoir of the Indian Mutiny, 1857* (1858). Also: *Asiatic Journal and Monthly Miscellany*, vol 19, p37; *Asiatic Journal and Monthly Register for British India*, for years 1820, 1825, 1833; *Bengal Obituary* (1851), p393; *Calcutta Magazine and Monthly Register*, incl 1831, pp. 147–148; *Lancet*, ed Thomas Wakley (1845); *Morning Chronicle* (London), 21.1.1824; *Oriental Herald and Journal of General Literature; Oriental Magazine and Calcutta Review; Parbury's Oriental Herald and Colonial Intelligencer; Sydney Morning Herald*, incl 15.2.1853, 20.10.1857, 12.10.1886, 30.12.1918; Families in British India Society (FIBIS) Database; 'Report from the Select Committee on Salt, British India; together with the minutes of evidence, and appendix', 1836; *www.law.mq.edu.au/research/colonial_case_law/colonial_cases/less_developed/calcutta/swetenham_v_macnaghten/*

Australia

G.H. Abbott, *Reminiscences of Newtown and Neighbourhood* (1937); *Australian Dictionary of Biography* – online edition; William Bampton, 'Journal of Captain William Bampton' (1793), copy of original at the State Library of New South Wales; George Blaikie, 'Mr Cuthbertson Shoots Through', *Western Mail* (Perth), 4.2.1954, pp. 8–9; Elizabeth Birch, 'The Bridal Banquet', originally in *Cavalcade*, 1946; Mary Phoebe Broughton, *Diary, 1839–1841*, SLNSW Call Number MLMSS 4010; Isadore Brodsky, *Sydney's Phantom Book Shops* (1973); Eileen Chanin, *Book Life – The Life and Times of David Scott Mitchell* (2011); William Chubb (ed), *Jubilee Souvenir of the Municipality of Newtown* (1912), p30; David Collins, *An Account of the English Colony in New South Wales* (1798); Dymphna Cusack, T. Inglis Moore, Barry Ovenden, Mary Gilmore – a Tribute (1965); G.F. Davidson, *Trade and Travel in the Far East* (1846), Chapter 3, 'New South Wales'; Edward Duyker, 'What the Dickens?', *National Library of Australia News*, February (1997), pp. 6–8; Shirley Fitzgerald, *Chippendale – Beneath the Factory Wall* (1990); William Freame, 'Dickens and Australia', *Parramatta and District Historical Society: Journal and Proceedings*, vol III (1923); John Godl, 'Remembering Camperdown Lodge – James Tyrrell's Reminiscences' (unpublished interview with Bill Bradshaw), 'The Donnithorne's [sic] of Camperdown Lodge' and miscellaneous papers, Marrickville Public Library, Sydney, NSW; John Gunn, *Along Parallel Lines: a history of the railways in New South Wales* (1989), p54; Baron Charles von Hügel, *New Holland Journal* (1994, translated and edited by Dymphna Clark); Margaret Kiddle, *Caroline Chisholm* (1950); Thomas Henry Huxley, *Letters and Diary 1850* (Huxley papers online); Robert Logan Jack, Chapter XVI 'The *Hormuzeer* and *Chesterfield* (Bampton and Alt)' in *Northmost Australia* (1921); Max Kelly (ed), *Nineteenth-Century Sydney* (1978); John Laws (with Christopher Stewart), *There's always more to the story* (2007); Robert Lehane, *Duelling Surgeon, Colonial Patriot – The Remarkable Life of William Bland* (2011); Ludwig Leichhardt, *Journal of an Overland Expedition in Australia, 1844–1845* (1846); James Maclehose, *Picture of Sydney and Strangers' Guide in N.S.W. for 1839* (1977); A.J. Marshall, *Darwin and Huxley in Australia* (1970); 'Miss Donnithorne's Maggot', Plots and Notes, New Chamber Opera (UK) website; Godfrey Charles Mundy, *Our Antipodes* (1852); Matt Murphy, 'The Truth about the Truth about Eliza Donnithorne', Sydney Archives Newtown Project website; Michael Nash, Chapter 1 'New South Wales and India', *Sydney Cove: The History and Archaeology of an Eighteenth-Century Shipwreck* (2009); The Newtown Project *www.sydneyarchives.info*; Robert H. Parr, 'Waiting for the Bridegroom', *Australasian Record* (Adventist Archives), 5.7.1976; J.O. Randall, *Pastoral Settlement in Northern Victoria: vol. II: The Campaspe District* (1982); J.S. Ryan, 'Donnithorne, Eliza Emily (1826?–1886)', Australian Dictionary of Biography, vol 4 (1972), p86 and 'A Possible Australian Source for Miss Havisham', *Australian Literary Studies*, vol 1, no 2, December 1963, pp. 134–136; Graham Seal, *Great Australian Stories* (2010); Paul de Serville, *Port Phillip Gentlemen and Good Society in Melbourne before the Gold Rushes* (1980); Alan Sharpe, *Newtown – Pictorial History* (1999); *Pictorial History – Manly to Palm Beach* (1993); Allan Sierp, *Colonial Life in New South Wales – Fifty Years of Photography 1855–1905* (1974); Babette Smith, *A Cargo of Women – Susannah Watson and the convicts of the Princess* Royal (2008); Anne Summers, *Damned Whores and God's Police* (1975); James Tyrrell, *Old Books, Old Friends, Old Sydney* (1987); W.H. Wilde, *Courage, a grace – a biography of Dame Mary Gilmore* (1988).

Also: William Bland – papers, 26 May 1817– 28 July 1868, State Library of New South Wales, Call Number DLMSQ 20 – DLMSQ 21; James Charles Cox – Records, Mitchell and Dixson Libraries Manuscripts Collection, State Libary of NSW, Ref UNCAT MSS 306; Stuart Alexander Donaldson – papers, 1829–1857, State Library of New South Wales, Call Number A 726 A 731; Donnithorne family – papers, State Library of NSW, Call Number M1713–1717; Dulhunty Papers, Chapters 8 and 9, www.dulhunty.com; The Lachlan & Elizabeth Macquarie Archive *www.library.mq.edu.au/digital/lema*; *Statement of the case of the pastoral tenants of the Crown in Victoria* (1856); State Library of Victoria: *Burke's Colonoial Gentry* 4th edn, 1863, vol 1, p381; Cooper Index; Kenyon Index; Billis and Kenyon, *Pastoral Pioneers of Port Phillip*, 2nd edn, 1974; *Kerr's Melbourne Almanac and Port Phillip Directory for 1841*, p241; Society of Australian Genealogists, Sydney; State Records of NSW; Trent University Archives; *Advertiser* (Adelaide), 21.8.1915, p15; *Argus* (Melbourne) 5.8.1875, p6, 16.1.1878, p9, 20.7.1940, p4, 11.2.1950, p25; *Bell's Life in Sydney and Sporting Reviewer*, 8.4.1848; *Brisbane Courier*, 1.3.1928, p20; *Daily Telegraph*, 23 August 1955; *Hawkesbury Herald*, 20.11.1903, p8; 'Our Metropolitan Suburbs: Newtown' in *Illustrated Sydney News* 27.6.1889, pp. 14–19, and *Illustrated Sydney News*, 27.6.1889, pp. 18–22; *Inquirer & Commercial News* (Perth, WA), 26.8.1889, p3; *Mercury* (Hobart), 3.8.1909, p3; 19.8.1927, p5; *Northhampton Chronicle and Echo* (UK), 16.12.2011; *Sun*, 11.12.1912; *Sunday Age*, 7.3.2004; *Sun Herald*, 1911; *Sunday Telegraph*, 18 August 1991, p94; *Sydney Herald*, 6.10.1841, p2 and 22.9.1846; *Sydney Morning Herald*, 13.2.1843, p3, 27.2.1843, p3, 8.10.1861, p3, 19.8.1887, p7, 11.9.1889, p4, 5.1.1935, p11, 31.7.1935, p10, 21.2.1948, p5, 3.2.1948, 11.11.1953, p2, 12.6.1954, p2; 11.11.2004; *Sydney Monitor*, 22 August 1838, p4; *Telegraph* (UK), 28.6.2008; *Truth*, 18.5.1924; *Western Mail*, 4 February, 1954, p8; *www.local-legends.net*

ACKNOWLEDGEMENTS

For their help I thank Suzanne Alder, Anthony Beckles Willson, Nelson Butler, Gabrielle Carey, Mridula Chakraborty, Sue Comrie-Thomson, Naomi Crago, Bill Davidson, Andrew Davies, Rose Docker, Carol Davies Foster, Barbara Dawson, Govert Deketh, Alan Donnithorne, Suzanne Falkiner, Elizabeth Fortescue, Alice Giles, John Godl, Paula Grunseit, Lynne Hadley, Colin Harris, Philip Heselton, Wendy Hibbitt, John Johnson, Clinton Johnston, Caroline Kades, Jonathan King, Karen Lambert, Robert Lehane, Mary Kay Mahoney, Alison Martyn, David McRuvie, Chrys Meader, Leonie Mickleborough, Matt Murphy, Faith Page, Simon Page, Toni Paramore, Melody Parker, Sarah Portley, Richard Pugh, Mick Reed, Marcelle Rodgers, Peter Rose, Rosemary Shepherd, Vivian Smith, Jennifer Strauss, Walter Struve, Anne Summers, Andrew Thom, Liz Thompson, Stella Vaughan, Edmund Walker, Robin Walsh, Sarah White, Harry Williamson, Pamela Wright, Russell Yeoman, and the librarians at the National Maritime Museum, the Mitchell Library and the National Library of Australia. Thanks especially to Jackie Cooper, for the sketch or *essay* of a lace collar, and to David Malouf for conversations about Sydney, writing and the past. For trusting me with their Donnithorne stories I thank Carol Moeser in Australia, Audrey Donnithorne in Hong Kong, and Anthea Gurkan in Turkey. Special thanks to Judy Barradell-Smith in England, for keeping me going with her enthusiasm and intelligence and sense of humour. Special thanks of a very personal kind to Sam Juers Indyk and Maya Robertson, Ben Juers Indyk and Bailey Sharp, and to Ursula Juers. Above all to Ivor Indyk, for love and books and for making it all happen.

This project has been assisted by the Commonwealth Government through the Australia Council, its arts funding and advisory body.